The Mill on the Floss

A Natural History

TWAYNE'S MASTERWORK STUDIES

Robert Lecker, General Editor

THE MILL ON THE FLOSS

A Natural History

Rosemary Ashton

Twayne Publishers • Boston
A Division of G. K. Hall & Co.

The Mill on the Floss: A Natural History
Rosemary Ashton

Twayne's Masterwork Studies No. 54
Copyright 1990 by G. K. Hall & Co.
All rights reserved.
Published by Twayne Publishers
A division of G. K. Hall & Co.
70 Lincoln Street, Boston, Massachusetts.

Copyediting supervised by Barbara Sutton.
Book production by Gabrielle B. McDonald.

Typeset in 10/14 Sabon by Compositors Corporation of Cedar Rapids, Iowa.

The paper used in this publication meets the minimum requirements of American National Standard for Information Sciences—Permanence of Paper for Printed Library Materials, ANSI Z39.48–1984. ∞

Printed and bound in the United States of America.

Library of Congress Cataloging-in-Publication Data

Ashton, Rosemary, 1947–
    The mill on the Floss : a natural history / Rosemary Ashton.
        p.   cm. — (Twayne's masterwork studies ; no. 54)
    A study of The mill on the Floss by George Elliot.
    Includes bibliographical references.
        1. Eliot, George, 1819–1880. Mill on the Floss. I. Title.
    II. Series.
    PR4664.A84   1990
    823'.8—dc20   90–30432
                                                                  CIP

0-8057-9406-9 (alk. paper) 10 9 8 7 6 5 4 3 2 1
0-8057-8134-X (pbk.: alk. paper) 10 9 8 7 6 5 4 3 2 1
First published 1990

To Ben, Katie, and Tom

Contents

Note on the References and Acknowledgments

For this study I have used the Penguin English Library edition of *The Mill on the Floss,* edited by A. S. Byatt (Harmondsworth: Penguin, 1979). It is based on the first edition of the novel (1860), collated with the manuscript in the British Library, and in a few cases the manuscript reading is restored. Where appropriate, I have described the variations in my notes. This edition is widely available in paperback, and therefore appropriate for students. In addition, the editor's decision to reprint from the manuscript and first edition is one with which I agree, especially because one of my chapters deals with the congruence of language and ideas between Charles Darwin and George Eliot, a congruence that is more evident in the manuscript than in subsequent versions of the novel. The frontispiece portrait of George Eliot is by Sir Frederic Burton (1865) and is reproduced by permission of the National Portrait Gallery, London.

George Eliot
Portrait by Frederic Burton. Courtesy of the National Portrait Gallery, London.

Chronology: George Eliot's Life and Works

1819   Mary Ann Evans born 22 November at South Farm, Arbury, Warwickshire, the third child of the second marriage of Robert Evans, estate manager to the Newdigate family of Arbury Hall, and Christiana Pearson.

1824   Brother, Isaac (b. 1816), goes to boarding school.

1828   Goes to school in Nuneaton, taught by Maria Lewis, who encourages her pupil in fervent evangelicalism.

1832   First Reform Bill passed, extending the franchise to the middle-class property owner.

1836   Mother dies 3 February. Mary Ann keeps house for her father.

1837   Queen Victoria ascends the throne.

1842   Under the influence of freethinking Coventry friends, the Brays and Hennells, Mary Ann refuses to accompany her father to church.

1844   Takes on the translation of David Friedrich Strauss's *Life of Jesus,* a rationalist account of the Gospels.

1846   *Life of Jesus* published anonymously by the radical publisher John Chapman.

1849   Father dies 6 June.

1850   Calls herself Marian Evans. After spending some months in Geneva, she settles in London, lodging at 142, Strand, with John Chapman. Becomes unpaid editor of the *Westminster Review,* owned by Chapman.

1851   Moves in London's radical circles, meeting philosophers, free-thinkers, and bohemians, including Herbert Spencer, John Stuart Mill, Harriet Martineau, and George Henry Lewes.

1854   Publishes her translation of Ludwig Feuerbach's *Essence of Christianity* under the name Marian Evans. Decides to live with

G. H. Lewes as his wife. He is already married to Agnes Jervis, who has borne three surviving sons to Lewes—Charles (b. 1842), Thornton (b. 1844), and Herbert (b. 1846)—and four children to his friend and cofounder of the *Leader* newspaper, Thornton Hunt. As Lewes has condoned the adultery, he cannot, under English law, divorce Agnes. Lewes and Marian travel to Weimar and Berlin to allow Lewes to complete his research for *The Life of Goethe* (1855).

1855 Returns to England in March and finds herself unacceptable in "respectable" female circles. Continues journalism for the *Westminster*.

1855–1856 Writes several incisive review articles on religion, history, and literature, most notably "The Natural History of German Life" and "Silly Novels by Lady Novelists," in which she declares that artistic realism and an extension of human sympathies by authors are the highest aims of literature.

1857 In *Blackwood's Magazine* publishes her first work of fiction, *Scenes of Clerical Life,* consisting of three stories, "The Sad Fortunes of the Reverend Amos Barton," "Mr. Gilfil's Love-Story," and "Janet's Repentance." Uses the pseudonym George Eliot for the first time. Her brother, Isaac, breaks off all contact with her when she tells him of her "marriage."

1859 First novel, *Adam Bede,* published 1 February. Sells more than 13,000 copies in the first year, and is favorably reviewed. Dickens admires it, as does Queen Victoria, who commissions two watercolors from Edward Corbould depicting scenes from the novel. Rumors about the identity of the author and false claims for a Mr. Liggins of Warwickshire. Starts writing *The Mill on the Floss* in January. Publishes a short story, "The Lifted Veil," in *Blackwood's Magazine* in July. Publication of Charles Darwin's *Origin of Species* November.

1860 *The Mill on the Floss* published 4 April as a "companion picture of provincial life" to follow *Adam Bede.*

1861 *Silas Marner* published.

1863 Publishes *Romola,* set in fifteenth-century Florence. Death of Thackeray, with whom George Eliot is frequently compared in contemporary reviews.

1864 Short story, "Brother Jacob," published in *Cornhill Magazine,* July.

1866 Returns to Blackwood, and to English provincial life in the recent past, with *Felix Holt, the Radical.*

Chronology

1867	Passing of the Second Reform Bill, further extending the male franchise.
1868	Publication of *The Spanish Gypsy*, a long poem showing the influence of Auguste Comte's positivist philosophy of the evolving stages of society and belief.
1869	Death of Lewes's son Thornie in October at the age of twenty-five. George Eliot has nursed him through a painful illness contracted in Africa, while beginning work on *Middlemarch*.
1870	Dickens dies. First Education Act to make free schooling compulsory for all children.
1873	*Middlemarch: A Study of Provincial Life* published, establishing George Eliot as the greatest novelist of the age. She is finally accepted in the best society, deemed fit to meet royalty.
1874	Publishes *The Legend of Jubal and Other Poems*. Includes a series of sonnets entitled "Brother and Sister," written in 1869, reminiscing about her relationship with Isaac and having a close connection to some of the childhood scenes in *The Mill on the Floss*.
1876	Her last novel, *Daniel Deronda*, published.
1878	Publishes *Impressions of Theophrastus Such*, a collection of moral and philosophical opinions and anecdotes. Lewes dies 30 November. Desolate, George Eliot reads Tennyson's *In Memoriam* for consolation.
1880	Marries John Cross, twenty years her junior, 6 May. Sends word to Isaac that she is legally married. He replies briefly with "sincere congratulations." George Eliot dies 22 December. Buried next to Lewes in Highgate Cemetery.

Chapter 1

Historical Context

The history of how Mary Ann Evans, daughter of a self-taught Midlands estate manager, came to be the wise, witty, cosmopolitan writer George Eliot is not only a particular—and particularly interesting—one, but also an illustration of several of the most important cultural trends of the century itself. She was born in rural Warwickshire in 1819. Her father and older brother Isaac belonged to that yeoman class that was declining as society became more industrialized and urbanized. A yeoman was, from medieval times to the later nineteenth century, when the class died out, an upper servant of royalty or nobility, a man respected and to some degree independent, often holding some land of his own. Robert Evans was such a man. A carpenter by trade—like Adam Bede—he rose to manage the large estates of Arbury Hall, home of the great Newdigate family.

Mary Ann received a respectable, if limited, education at boarding schools in the area. While the curriculum was narrow enough—English, French, history, arithmetic, with some music and drawing—her teachers, and, more important, her father encouraged her to read widely. He even allowed her to have Italian and German lessons from a tutor, Joseph Brezzi, when she left school after her mother's death in 1836 and came

1

home to be her father's housekeeper. Already she was showing signs of a prodigious appetite for learning.

The religion of the Evans family was the low form of the Church of England, but Mary Ann herself came under the influence of the extreme evangelical wing of the established church and had direct experience of the dissenting religions that had taken a hold over certain sections of the English lower and middle classes since the later eighteenth century. Her father's brother, Samuel Evans, was married to a Methodist lay preacher, who was to provide George Eliot with material for her portrayal of Dinah Morris in *Adam Bede*. Her earliest mentor, the teacher Maria Lewis, was a fervent evangelical under whose influence the teenage Mary Ann, like the teenage Maggie Tulliver, renounced ordinary secular pleasures such as novel reading and theater going. This extreme severity was short-lived, however, soon giving way to a view of religion much more offensive to her more orthodox father and brother than her previous excessive piety. In 1840 she and her father had moved closer to Coventry, one of the many rapidly expanding provincial towns in which a philanthropic and politically progressive manufacturing middle class was becoming increasingly the dominant social and cultural group. Here Mary Ann met the family of Charles Bray, a ribbon manufacturer. Her intercourse with the Brays, and their in-laws the Hennells, broadened her education and her views, with the result that by 1842 she was refusing to attend church with her father, having embraced their freethinking in religious matters.

While Methodism and other dissenting creeds had been winning souls from a complacent and worldly Church of England during the past seventy years, a contrary trend had also been making headway, though more slowly and chiefly among the educated middle class. Historical researches into biblical texts, particularly in Germany, where there had been an extraordinary flourishing of comparative studies of languages and cultures since the 1790s, led to difficulties among historians and theologians about taking many scriptural passages as literally true. The comparative study of myths showed that many ancient cultures cherished stories of creation, floods, and other cataclysmic events parallel to those told in the Old Testament. Dating of biblical books became problematic. Mary Ann Evans's reading, particularly of her friend Charles Hennell's

Historical Context

Inquiry into the Origins of Christianity (1838) and David Friedrich Strauss's *Das Leben Jesu* (1835–36), convinced her of the mythical nature of biblical texts and induced her to adopt a humanist creed from which she never again departed. In 1844 she took over from Hennell's wife the translation of Strauss's *Life of Jesus*, which was brought out by the radical publisher John Chapman in 1846.

Thus a young woman, living in the provinces and partly self-educated, mediated the work that did more than any other book to unsettle a generation of young men at Oxford and Cambridge. Arthur Hugh Clough, Matthew Arnold's older brother Tom, J. A. Froude, and Samuel Butler are perhaps the best known of a whole generation of university students who were cut adrift from their religious moorings in the 1840s and 1850s, and whose chosen careers as university dons were closed to them by their inability to remain in the established church and subscribe to its creeds. Mary Ann Evans was now a precocious member of that typical and powerful class, the mid-Victorian intelligentsia. As George Eliot, she was to represent in her fiction the urbane, progressive, intellectually skeptical, decidedly cosmopolitan rather than national or provincial, voice of her age. Interestingly, especially with reference to *The Mill on the Floss*, she often exercised her large mind in illustrating and analyzing the very life of her past—provincial, traditional, pious—against which she had, alone among her family, rebelled. Her characteristic mixed tone of irony combined with large tolerance is the result of her progressive learning tempered by a loyalty of feeling toward her past. The Dodson and Tulliver families in *The Mill on the Floss* are mercilessly analyzed and criticized, yet also lovingly rendered.

After her father's death in 1849 Marian Evans, as she now began to call herself, boldly moved to London to create an independent career. She lodged with Chapman, becoming his editorial adviser in the running of the influential radical periodical, the *Westminster Review*. In a series of amazingly confident and mature essays for the *Review* she dealt with all the burning intellectual issues of the day—rationalism, philosophical history, geology, natural science—as well as reviewing contemporary fiction. She was forming a view that literature and art could best serve humanity's needs by attempting a realism of presentation, particularly of

3

ordinary, unheroic people. In "The Natural History of German Life" (July 1856) she stated her creed, supported by examples from Sir Walter Scott and Wordsworth, that art ought to achieve "the extension of our sympathies." "Art," she wrote, "is the nearest thing to life. . . . We want to be taught to feel, not for the heroic artisan or the sentimental peasant, but for the peasant in all his coarse apathy, and the artisan in all his suspicious selfishness."[1] In *Lyrical Ballads* Wordsworth had solicited our interest and sympathy for poor widows, struggling farmers, and old men eking out hard livings, and Scott had given true-to-life scenes in peasant cottages, daring to use the colorful language and broad dialect of his fellow lowland Scots. These were to be the literary examples she followed in her early novels set in the heart of rural England.

Such a literary creed evolved naturally enough in harmony with Marian Evans's embracing of the "religion of humanity" propounded by the social philosopher Auguste Comte and the philosopher-historian Ludwig Feuerbach. "Homo homini deus est," "the essence of Christianity is the essence of human feeling," "the first object of man is man," "the consciousness of God is nothing else than the consciousness of the species"[2]—by these striking phrases Feuerbach announced in *Das Wesen des Christenthums* (1841) his belief that Christianity is a fiction made by man to express symbolically his moral relations with his fellow men. Who else but Marian Evans, already the translator of Strauss, should render this work into English? Her translation appeared under the title *The Essence of Christianity* in July 1854. In the same month she took the bold step of going to live with a married man, G. H. Lewes, a radical freethinker like herself. They traveled to Weimar and Berlin, where he finished his research for the biography of Goethe he had been planning for several years.

Goethe was an important figure for George Eliot too. In a short essay, "The Morality of *Wilhelm Meister*" (July 1855), she praised his lack of overt moral comment or direction, arguing that his very refusal always to reward the good and punish the wicked is moral because true to life: "He quietly follows the stream of fact and of life; and waits patiently for the moral processes of nature as we all do for her material processes."[3] The language here is that of evolution, a doctrine foreshadowed in

Historical Context

Goethe's amateur scientific studies and embraced by Lewes, also a keen natural historian, and George Eliot. Darwin's *Origin of Species,* which appeared late in 1859 while George Eliot was finishing *The Mill on the Floss,* represented the culmination of the theory of gradual development according to physical laws with which George Eliot and G. H. Lewes were familiar from their reading and their nature studies. *The Mill on the Floss* is studded with Darwinian metaphors referring to the successful, or otherwise, efforts of individuals to adapt to an ever-changing environment.

All George Eliot's novels are concerned with the interrelatedness of individuals both to one another and to their social "medium." None is more insistently a "natural history" than *The Mill on the Floss* with its ethnographic analysis of gradual social change and its description—part comic, part tragic—of the stages of adaptation and the variations from the parent stock of the different generations of the Dodson and Tulliver families. For George Eliot, as for Darwin, the doctrine of "natural selection" and the "struggle for life" is not exclusively optimistic. Survival of the fittest is a grim law, for it is not synonymous with survival of the best. *The Mill on the Floss* roots the individual tragedy of Maggie within a general sense of "the onward tendency of human things."[4] It provides an exciting imaginative illustration of the most important philosophical and scientific theories of the mid-nineteenth century.

Chapter 2

The Importance of the Work

"By God she is a *wonderful* woman." So spoke George Eliot's publisher, John Blackwood, on reading the penultimate chapter of *The Mill on the Floss* in March 1860. In his encouraging way he had written regularly to his diffident, often desponding, author, giving her his response to the work as it progressed. Of *The Mill on the Floss* he now wrote, "I await with trembling impatience the Catastrophe," and he assured her that "The Mill on the Floss is safe for immortality."[1]

Blackwood was right. We still read the novel and marvel at its author's genius. Though a less fully accomplished work than her masterpiece, *Middlemarch,* and perhaps less fresh than her first novel, *Adam Bede,* the general favorite among her contemporaries, *The Mill on the Floss* has unique claims on our attention. Its peculiar combination of autobiographical truth of feeling (often painful feeling), broad ironic humor, exciting plotting, and final tragic catastrophe marks it out as special, not only among George Eliot's novels, but also as a fine example of the Victorian novel—the species to which it belongs—and of the genus novel itself. The nineteenth-century novel has been the subject of heated critical debate in recent years. Deconstructionist critics write rather dismissively of the "classic realist novel" with its inevitable tendency to embody (albeit unconsciously) an outmoded capitalist ideology. Meanwhile, ordinary members of the reading public, and a large part of the scholarly and critical readership too, are resistant to such reductive readings.

What, we may ask, do most readers expect of a novel, and how does *The Mill on the Floss* satisfy their requirements? As the novel, unlike a lyric poem or a drama, has a primarily narrative structure and is extensive, both in the sense of taking up many pages and in covering long periods of "novel time"—in short, as the novel has taken over the function of epic, the telling of a story at leisure—readers generally expect that it will strike them as, in some sense, like "real" life. The exceptions to this—great jeux d'esprit like *Tristram Shandy* or James Joyce's *Ulysses,* both written partly to turn orthodox realism on its head—only reinforce the rule. We want of a novel a good story well told, with characters with whom we are imaginatively engaged. This expectation is not so naive as it may at first sight appear. Readers know that novels are plotted, have a pattern, are linguistic structures, consist of a beginning, a middle, and an end, and are the product of an artistic consciousness working within the contexts of a literary tradition and a particular historical period. In these respects, novels are not exactly "like life." Yet we judge them partly on their ability to render imaginary constructs with a concreteness and energy suggestive of life itself.

Certainly George Eliot wished her readers to respond to her creations in this way. She herself wept over Maggie and Tom as she wrote the last volume of *The Mill on the Floss*. As Lewes reported to Blackwood, "Mrs. Lewes is getting her eyes redder and *swollener* every morning as she lives through her tragic story," adding shrewdly, "the more she cries, and the readers cry, the better say I."[2] Her artistic creed formed part of her general philosophical outlook, in that she thought literature generally, and "social novels" in particular, ought to widen human sympathies, "amplifying experience and extending our contact with our fellow-men beyond the bounds of our personal lot."[3] She achieves her object in *The Mill on the Floss* partly by appealing to feelings that we will find it easy to share: our natural sympathy for children as they go through the exciting but often perplexing process of growing up in adult society. Like

Wordsworth, she draws directly on her own memories, and, like him, she asks us to respond from the depths of our own half-remembered past. Her vividly realized scenes in the early part of the novel—Maggie and Tom fishing and quarreling, eating jam puffs and quarreling, entering on forbidden territory together and quarreling—have their specific content, but are also generally true to childhood experience. They strike us, in Keats's phrase for great poetry, as "almost a remembrance."

Partly, and this is the more difficult task, George Eliot achieves her aim by persuading us to sympathize with characters less attractive than the children. Mr. Tulliver is hot-headed, foolish, and litigious; as a result, he gets into financial trouble and is finally ruined. But we are not encouraged to gloat. By expert plotting and by using the language of webs and connections, George Eliot shows how he is only partly responsible for his own destiny. Things turn out for him as they do, "not because Mr. Tulliver's will was feeble, but because external fact was stronger" (198). The author invokes both the tragic and the comic modes in her delineation of the ups and downs of "these emmet-like Dodsons and Tullivers" with their "prosaic form of human life," their adherence to narrow customs (362–63).

The novel delights us with its extraordinary range of linguistic description. There is the pervasive language of evolution, even the direct evocation of natural history: "does not science tell us that its highest striving is after the ascertainment of a unity which shall bind the smallest things with the greatest?" (363). This language is ingeniously combined with references to Greek tragedy: "Mr. Tulliver had a destiny as well as Oedipus, and in this case he might plead, like Oedipus, that his deed was inflicted on him rather than committed by him" (198). And there is the colorful, direct language of the rustic characters themselves. When Mr. Tulliver wishes to override his wife's objection to sending Tom to a particular school on the grounds that it is too far away for her to do his weekly washing, he says, "you mustn't put a spoke i' the wheel about the washin', if we can't get a school near enough. That's the fault I have to find wi' you, Bessy: if you see a stick i' the road, you're allays thinkin' you can't step over it" (57).

The Mill on the Floss engages our sympathy for characters attractive and unattractive. It offers rich comedy in the portraits of the Dodson sisters, expertly plotted tragedy in the unintentional mutual thwarting of each other's purposes by Tom and Maggie (mirroring their parents' tragicomic relationship), and it links both the tragedy and the comedy to an analysis of the progress of human society as it evolves economically and educationally in the early part of the nineteenth century in which the novel is set. To imply, however, that it represents Darwinism fictionalized is to suggest something too narrow and schematized. *The Mill on the Floss* is rather an imaginative embodiment of the most progressive thinking of its time. It is also a problematic work, puzzling in its comedy and tragedy, sometimes ambivalent in tone, deeply melancholy in spite of the narrator's emphasis on progress, and, above all, with its close relation to the sore spots of its author's life, very strongly felt.

Chapter 3

Critical Reception

Scenes of Clerical Life and Adam Bede were fine embodiments of George Eliot's belief, elaborated in her essays of the mid-1850s, that art should embrace "*realism*—the doctrine that all truth and beauty are to be attained by a humble and faithful study of nature, and not by substituting vague forms, bred by imagination on the mists of feeling, in place of definite, substantial reality."[1] On the assumption that art is at its most truthful (and moral) when it seizes our interest and engages our emotions with "palpably and unmistakably commonplace" people like Amos Barton ("The Sad Fortunes of the Reverend Amos Barton," chapter 5), in the way that Flemish art attracts our attention to "those old women scraping carrots" (*Adam Bede,* chapter 17), George Eliot had thus set out to correct what she saw as a deplorable trend in Victorian fiction. Though she admired Dickens for his "power of rendering the external traits of our town population," she regretted his inability to depict the "psychological character" of that population without becoming "as transcendent in his unreality as he was a moment before in his artistic truthfulness."[2]

In an amusing survey of "Silly Novels by Lady Novelists" (October 1856) she singled out as one type of silly novel "the *white neck-cloth* species," in which evangelical tracts are dressed up as fiction, pandering to the lowest reading taste by suggesting that evangelicalism is invariably genteel, well-dressed, romantic, and fashionable. "The real drama of Evangelicalism," she wrote, "—and it has abundance of fine drama for anyone who has genius enough to discern and reproduce it—lies among the middle and lower classes."[3] By the time this article was published, in October 1856, George Eliot had begun her own first story of lower- and middle-class evangelical life, "Amos Barton." Soon after came *Adam Bede.* The reading public responded well. Dickens was generous in his praise, and after *Adam Bede* he solicited the unknown author to publish her next novel in his periodical *All the Year Round,* avowing that he would be delighted "to have such an artist working with me." Kind Mrs. Gaskell wrote, "I have had the greatest compliment paid me I ever had in my life. I have been suspected of having written 'Adam Bede.'"[4] The novel sold over thirteen thousand copies in the first year and established "George Eliot" as an exciting new name on the literary scene. What would the next novel be like?

By the time *The Mill on the Floss* appeared in April 1860, "all England" was "on tiptoe with expectation," Lewes wrote to his son Charles in Switzerland.[5] The curiosity arose partly because it was now generally known, against the wishes of author and publisher, that "George Eliot" was the "strong-minded woman"[6] and translator of Strauss who was living in an irregular relationship with G. H. Lewes. A persistent rumor, begun in the Midlands, where local people recognized "portraits" in *Scenes of Clerical Life* and *Adam Bede,* had it that a certain Joseph Liggins was the author. Mr. Liggins inconveniently omitted to deny the story. In London, Herbert Spencer, John Chapman, and other literary friends began guessing at the authorship until there was nothing for it but to let the secret out. The reluctant Blackwood feared that sales of the new novel would be adversely affected, particularly since Charles Mudie of the famous circulating library, much depended on by publishers of novels, was known to be prudish. Lewes was anxious, too, though he preferred to voice a more general worry. "There is immense expectation," he wrote to a friend in March 1860, "and of course a very strong disposition to find that the book is a 'falling-off'—second books always have to go through *that.*"[7] The novel sold quickly at first, more than four thousand copies being bought in the first four days after publication, though over the longer term sales were slightly below those of *Adam Bede*. The critical reception of *The Mill on the Floss* was more varied than the chorus of approval that had greeted *Adam Bede*, as befitted a work that was in many ways more complex and ambitious than its predecessor.

How did George Eliot herself view her third attempt at fiction? She broached the subject with Blackwood in March 1859, telling him that her new story would be "as long as Adam Bede, and a sort of companion picture of provincial life." Later, comparing *The Mill on the Floss* to *Adam Bede*, she thought that though her first novel had been "better balanced," there was "more thought" in the second.[8] Perhaps she had in mind the guiding role of the narrator relating a "natural history" of an English provincial town in terminology borrowed from geology and biology. For the narrator is both historian and scientific analyst. Years later George Eliot's friend Emily Davies reported a conversation with the author about her philosophical aim in writing *The Mill on the Floss*: it was "to show the conflict which is going on everywhere when the younger generation with its higher culture comes into collision with the older."[9]

Many early reviewers noticed the terminology of "development," but in general they concentrated on George Eliot's scene painting and characterization. There was universal praise for her vivid depiction of childhood fears and desires. E. S. Dallas of the *Times* (London), who began his review with the sentence, "'George Eliot' is as great as ever," thought that no one had, before this, "ventured to paint the childlife in all its prosaic reality"; the *Spectator* critic declared her "gift of knowing the child-soul in those things which are common to all children" far superior to Dickens's.[10] Henry James's view was that of all the pictures of childhood to be found in English novels, none was "more truthful and touching than the early pages of this work."[11] The most intelligent of George Eliot's critics did more than merely marvel at her gift for inhabiting children's minds and rendering dramatic scenes of childhood; they noted, usually with admiration tinged with regret, that such scenes, though humorous and pathetic, form part of a pattern suggestive of a melancholy view of the inevitability of change and progress and of individual struggle. As Dallas observed, "Everybody in this tale is repelling everybody, and life is in the strictest sense a battle."

The portrayal of the older generation, the Dodsons and Tullivers, produced conflicting reactions. It was recognized that they were drawn with masterly skill and humor, and many critics chuckled over scenes in which Maggie's aunts solemnly unlock cupboards to reveal a new hat or a cherished wedding gift, or argue over the best way to educate Tom or to save Mr. Tulliver from bankruptcy. But the same critics often demurred over the selfishness of these "odious" Dodsons (Dallas's word). The shrewd Blackwood, reading the novel as it arrived in manuscript installments, told George Eliot how he and his family laughed over the scenes with the Dodson sisters, but he delicately hinted that he found their hardness toward Mr. Tulliver in his financial trouble somewhat oppressive: "The scenes in these pages are painted with a power and minute finish which is perfectly wonderful. I entered so keenly into the matter and felt so angry at the Dodson sisterhood that I could hardly laugh at their absurdities, intensely comical as they are. I wish you could have given them some touch of feeling to relieve the sensation of oppression."[12]

George Eliot was alarmed at the strength of animosity her readers felt against the sisters: "I have certainly fulfilled my intention very badly if I have made the Dodson honesty appear 'mean and uninteresting' . . . and I am so very far from hating the Dodsons myself, that I am rather aghast to find them ticketed with such very ugly adjectives."[13] Critics did have some reason to feel thus ambivalent about the Dodsons, however, since George Eliot herself gives out opposing signals about them through the narrator, who laughs at them for their individual vagaries while generally admiring, or half-admiring, their family closeness.

On the whole, contemporary readers and critics were ecstatic about the first two-thirds of the novel—"the very noblest of tragic as well as of humorous prose idyls [*sic*] in the language," as Swinburne said.[14] What really set them in a flutter was the last volume, in which Maggie, now a young woman, becomes half-engaged to Philip Wakem but is seduced into a near-elopement with Stephen Guest, who is himself unofficially engaged to Maggie's cousin Lucy Deane. Maggie returns home, having renounced Stephen, but in social disgrace, and the novel ends on a dramatic and symbolic note, with Maggie and her brother united after their estrangement, but only in death by the flood that sweeps through St. Ogg's. The problems faced by critics are three-fold. They concern the structure and balance of the novel as a whole; the morality and probability (not the same thing) of the denouement; and the appropriateness of the tragic ending. Victorian responses to these questions differ in some respects from modern ones, but that these are the problematic areas has been accepted equally by George Eliot's contemporaries and by their modern successors.

Concerning the first point, Sir Edward Bulwer-Lytton was the first of many readers to point out that the slow narrative of Maggie's and Tom's childhood gives way too suddenly to the crisis and drama of their young adulthoods. There is, he thought, insufficient preparation. George Eliot replied to this criticism, admitting its justice. She wrote revealingly: "The *epische Breite* [epic breadth] into which I was beguiled by love of my subject in the two first volumes, caused a want of proportionate fullness in the treatment of the third, which I shall always regret."[15] Richard Holt Hutton saw the novel as falling into two unequal parts: "a masterly fragment of fictitious biography in two volumes, followed by a second-rate one-volume novel."[16] Modern readers, too, may feel a jarring effect as they move with little warning (though there is, in fact, some preparation) from the earthy, comic milieu of lower-middle-class life among the Dodsons and Tullivers into volume 3, with its change of scene and of tone. George Eliot herself may well have felt uneasy here, for her description in the opening chapter of the last volume of the leisurely chatter and music making in Lucy Deane's "well-furnished drawing-room" hovers between neutrality and satire.

Virginia Woolf felt that George Eliot was "out of her element" when "forced to set foot in middle-class drawing-rooms where young men sing all the summer morning and young women sit embroidering smoking-caps for bazaars."[17] Her remark, though shrewd in terms of the unity of the novel, is snobbishly wide of the mark with regard to the kind of society known to George Eliot in 1860. It does, however, point to an important change at this juncture of the novel: George Eliot is moving out of scenes drawn directly from her own childhood experience, and there is a consequent loss of the intensity of that recollected past.

Few critics have been content with Stephen Guest. He makes his appearance too late to be completely credible as an important element in the drama to come. Moreover, how could George Eliot let Maggie be attracted to such a "thing" (Swinburne), a "mere hairdresser's block" (Leslie Stephen), a "sad lapse" on George Eliot's part (Leavis)?[18] This question provides a bridge between the problem of structural balance and the even more vexed one of the morality of Maggie's falling in love with Stephen. Some contemporary critics thought it immoral because improbable. How could noble Maggie even temporarily give way to the seductive arguments and (to the reader, if not to Maggie) dubious charms of this young man? This was Bulwer-Lytton's chief objection to the novel. Others, conversely, while accepting that in real life admirable women do sometimes fall in love with nonentities and scoundrels, held that this hardly made its depiction in a novel morally acceptable. The *Westminster* reviewer thus took George Eliot to task for being realistic to the exclusion of inculcating a proper morality: "Why did she love Guest? . . . George Eliot will no doubt say, why does any one love another? . . . The influence exercised by the sexes over each other is quite incalculable, is determined by no rules, is what the Germans call *daemonisch,* and beyond the sphere of reason. This is true enough in life, beneath whose surface we can penetrate to so small a depth, but in books we look for some indication of the affinities of choice."[19]

The complexity of this critical problem has not diminished. Post-Freudian critics usually eschew the question of morality, strictly viewed, in favor of explaining Maggie's "fall" deterministically (in this Darwinism and Freudianism are in harmony), and they also tend to transfer their common concern from Maggie's motivation to George Eliot's own. Thus Leavis talks of Maggie as a "self-idealization" of George Eliot herself, tinged with self-pity. Maggie is beautiful, where George Eliot is not; both hunger for love and attention.[20] In Leavis's view George Eliot is not aware that she has made Stephen unworthy of Maggie. Barbara Hardy, also pursuing a psychological argument available to modern critics conscious not only of Freud but also of the facts of George Eliot's life and the autobiographical nature of *The Mill on the Floss* (at which her contemporaries could only guess—as some of them did), seeks to explain the Maggie-Stephen relationship as a displacement of the George Eliot-Lewes one.[21]

While Victorian critics were puzzled and repelled by the quasi-elopement of Maggie and Stephen, they usually accepted the death of Tom and Maggie with equanimity, though there was the general sense of the catastrophe coming too suddenly, following too hard upon the long exposition. After the episode with Stephen, critics felt some relief at Maggie's death. The *Saturday Review* critic was "not sorry" to have the two principal characters "drowned off" after the upheavals of volume 3.[22] Modern readers, on the other hand, have been less troubled about the morality of the Maggie and Stephen episode, though there is still a need to answer Blackwood's intelligent question, put when he was reading that episode: "Why the devil is she putting poor Maggie into a position where she would be more than human if she did not come to grief?"[23] Attention has in this century focused on the outcome of Maggie's relationship with her brother. The psychological approach is predominant: the "Liebestod" of Maggie and Tom is a piece of wish fulfillment on George Eliot's part, with unrelenting Isaac Evans the loved and hated brother to be symbolically embraced and killed.[24] In the discussion of the novel that follows I address these concerns, paying attention also to those elements—Maggie's exclusion, as a girl, from receiving a stimulating education or finding an occupation worthy of her talents and aspirations—that have led many recent critics to approach the novel from a feminist point of view.[25]

A Reading

Chapter 4

Realism

We have already seen that George Eliot was, at the very beginning of her career as a novelist, a committed and self-confessed "realist." She meant by the term an artist who values the truth of observation above the imaginative fancies of writers of "romance" or fashionable melodramatic fiction. Not that the realist should eschew imagination; on the contrary, the observation of an object ought to be accompanied by an imaginative effort to extend the reader's or spectator's sympathies. Hence the stress, in her essays in the mid-1850s, on the need for "genuine observation" in place of the representation, found in the various subspecies of "silly novels" with which the public was regularly regaled, of fashionable millinery and ideal sentiment. Like Wordsworth, then, who had also battled against contemporary taste in his *Lyrical Ballads* (1798), she endeavored always to "look steadily at her subject."[1] This naturally entailed, for both Wordsworth and George Eliot, drawing liberally on their own experience. For both it was a matter of importance to show human beings in all their commonness, to illuminate and celebrate the "working-day business of the world."[2] Thus Wordsworth's poems deal with the everyday lives of farmers and shepherds, and *Adam Bede* begins, famously and unusually for its time, with a chapter entitled "The Workshop," in which Adam and his fellow carpenters are making a door.

Realistic treatment of characters was partly a matter of fidelity to fact in order to avoid absurdities such as the passage quoted by George Eliot in "Silly Novels" from Lady Chatterton's novel *Compensation,* ironically enough subtitled "A Story of Real Life Thirty Years Ago." In that work a child of four and a half years old talks in the following "Ossianic fashion":

"Oh, I am so happy, dear gran'mamma;—I have seen,—I have seen such a delightful person: he is like everything beautiful,—like the smell of sweet flowers, and the view from Ben Lomond;—or no, *better than that*—he is like what I think of and see when I am very, very happy; and he is really like mamma, too, when she sings; and his forehead is like *that distant sea,*" she continued, pointing to the blue Mediterranean; "there seems no end—no end; or like the clusters of stars I like best to look at on a warm fine night . . . Don't look so . . . your forehead is like Loch Lomond, when the wind is blowing and the sun is gone in; I like the sunshine best when the lake is smooth . . . So now—I like it better than ever . . . it is more beautiful still from the dark cloud that has gone over it, *when the sun suddenly lights up all the colours of the forests and shining purple rocks, and it is all reflected in the waters below.*"

George Eliot comments delightedly on this: "We are not surprised to learn that the mother of this infant phenomenon, who exhibits symptoms so alarmingly like those of adolescence repressed by gin, is herself a phoenix. We are assured, again and again, that she had a remarkably original mind, that she was a genius, and 'conscious of her originality,' and she was fortunate enough to have a lover who was also a genius, and a man of 'most original mind.'"[3]

Important though it is to avoid such silliness, there is a more pressing moral imperative in choosing to portray probabilities rather than improbabilities in novels. The convenient death of an inconvenient elderly husband, thus paving the way for the heroine, now rich, to marry the handsome young hero, is neither likely to happen in real life nor likely to inculcate moral feelings in a reader. When Geraldine Jewsbury, in her novel *Constance Herbert* (reviewed by George Eliot in July 1855), thinks she is illustrating a principle of duty by means of her romantic plot, she is wrong. There is nothing moral about three women giving up lovers, only to find that they were anyway "good for nothing": "The notion that duty looks stern, but all the while has her hand full of sugar-plums, with which she will reward us by-and-by, is the favourite cant of optimists, who try to make out that this tangled wilderness of life has a plan as easy to trace as that of a Dutch garden; but it really undermines all true moral development by perpetually substituting something extrinsic as a motive to action, instead of the immediate impulse of love or justice, which alone makes an action truly moral."[4] We shall see that this argument has some bearing on George Eliot's handling of Maggie's renunciation of Stephen in *The Mill on the Floss.*

It should be clear that her embracing of a realist creed is the result of more than a simple decision to write from experience rather than imagination. But the embracing of realism brings problems for the writer. Mere faithful recounting of actuality might, after all, so easily lead to shapelessness in the work of art. Wordsworth did not altogether escape this pitfall in *Lyrical Ballads* and in his long and often pedestrian poem, *The Excursion.* In "Amos Barton" George Eliot runs the risk of carrying on too long with mere description of the humdrum lives of Amos and his parishioners. As if sensing this, she rather abruptly introduces some excitement, thus incurring the problem of narrative imbalance. When drama—not unknown in life and a necessary part of the novelist's art—does come, it comes in a rush at the end, with the death of Milly Barton and the disgrace of Amos tumbling over each other. *Adam Bede,* too, has a rather conventional "romance" ending, with Arthur Donnithorne riding up at the eleventh hour bearing Hetty's pardon from the gallows. This sits oddly with the slow, "natural" growth of the plot hitherto. Scott, George Eliot's favorite novelist, had been guilty in the same way of topping off realism with romance. *The Mill on the Floss* also contains a contrast between the pastoral epic of its first two volumes and the turbulence of its third. The danger for novelists is thus to find themselves either writing melodrama or producing novels that are almost plotless, or moving abruptly from one mode into the other. Realist writers at their best combine experience with imagination, pace their narrative with care to include some crises, and exhibit a pattern of plot and imagery that pleases the reader's artistic sense without requiring his sense of probability to be completely suppressed. Most readers have felt that *The Mill on the Floss* is not fully successful in achieving this balance. (It is a question I discuss in chapter 8.)

Where George Eliot is most notably successful in her novel is in her psychological realism. As her contemporaries at once appreciated, she outshone even Jane Austen in her ability to penetrate appearances to dissect human motive and so persuade us that a given character would, or at least could, act in the way shown. Her children squabble and giggle, rather than talk in purple prose or show qualities impossibly saintly, like Dickens's little Paul Dombey. Maggie's sensitivity to adult scoldings she feels to be unjust, her rushing up to the attic to stick pins in her doll, cut her hair, or just sulk; Tom's argumentativeness over his belongings (rabbits, jam puffs, pocketknives); and both children's constant sense of puzzlement at the rituals and negative injunctions of the adults on whom they depend—all these are wonderfully true to everyone's experience of the childhood state.

George Eliot renders such scenes with great skill. Like Wordsworth, she does childhood the honor of taking it seriously. Not only are the children's feelings minutely analyzed and understood, but our sympathy is enlisted on their side against a largely unsympathetic adult environment. This is achieved by treating the grown-ups with irony and the children with none. For example, their disobedience of orders not to go out of bounds at Aunt Pullet's farm is set against adult restrictiveness taken to limits not far short of the caricaturable:

> Uncle Pullet had seen the expected party approaching from the window, and made haste to unbar and unchain the front door, kept always in this fortified condition from fear of tramps who might be supposed to know of the glass-case of stuffed birds in the hall and to contemplate rushing in and carrying it away on their heads. Aunt Pullet too appeared at the doorway, and as soon as her sister was within hearing said, "Stop the children, for God's sake, Bessy—don't let 'em

come up the door-steps: Sally's bringing the old mat and the duster, to
rub their shoes."

Mrs. Pullet's front-door mats were by no means intended to wipe
shoes on: the very scraper had a deputy to do its dirty work. (148)

Humor at the expense of the older generation is thus employed to
set off the agonies of the younger, and the psychology of both is shrewdly
laid bare. What can be more natural than that children so hedged about
by injunctions not to bring in dirt, drop crumbs, or break ornaments
should head straight for the forbidden part of the farm the moment they
are let loose? And what more common—even if here presented in an extreme form—than that members of one's extended family should allow
such inflexible habits of mind as excessive house-pride or fear of burglars
to dominate their speech and actions? Critics, though reveling in the
doleful excesses of the Dodson aunts, at the same time took George Eliot
to task for making them so hideous. Her immediate response was to be
"aghast" that "payment of one's debts" should be thought a "con-
temptible virtue." "So far as my own feeling and intention are concerned,
no one class of persons or form of character is held up to reprobation or
to exclusive admiration," she told William Blackwood, the brother of her
publisher.[5] Though one cannot doubt her sincerity, it remains true that in
her loving memorializing of childhood she has been led into rendering
adulthood unattractive. Yet she ought to be given the last word here. If
Maggie and Tom belong to her own past experience, so also do the
Dodsons, drawn in part from her mother's sisters. In 1869 she told Emily
Davies, in answer to the question whether she had known actual people
like the Dodsons, "Oh, so much worse." In her view everything is "sof-
tened" in *The Mill on the Floss* as compared with real life. Her own experience had been harsher.[6] It is a case of life throwing up characters quite
as peculiar as those any novelist's imagination could conjure, and readers
should beware of making too hastily the charge of caricature or exaggera-
tion. One might compare here the figure of Mr. Micawber in *David
Copperfield,* who seems impossibly larger than life until one learns of the

extravagant notions and actual diction of his real-life model, Dickens's own father.

Indeed, humor and realism are happily combined in *The Mill on the Floss*, partly by means of George Eliot's use of something close to dialect. It is not a simple matter of mocking the naïveté of the country bumpkin by making him speak something other than standard English, a device familiar at least since Shakespeare, though there is an element of the educated narrator recounting local speech and attitudes with benign superiority. Like Scott, from whom she took courage to attempt the transcription of a dialect unfamiliar to the mass of middle-class readers (doubtless Thomas Hardy took encouragement in turn from George Eliot's example), she used dialect to give a sense of felt life. She had already made clear in one of her essays her sense of the historical importance of local peculiarities of speech as carrying within them the true life of particular places at particular moments. In an argument close to Wordsworth's in his preface to *Lyrical Ballads,* she declared:

> Suppose, then, that the effort which has been again and again made to construct a universal language on a rational basis has at length succeeded, and that you have a language which has no uncertainty, no whims of idiom, no cumbrous forms, no fitful shimmer of many-hued significance, no hoary archaisms "familiar with forgotten years"—a patent deodorized and non-resonant language, which effects the purpose of communication as perfectly and rapidly as algebraic signs. Your language may be a perfect medium of expression to science, but will never express *life,* which is a great deal more than science. With the anomalies and inconveniences of historical language, you will have parted with its music and its passion, with its vital qualities as an expression of individual character, with its subtle capabilities of wit, with everything that gives it power over the imagination; and the next step in simplification will be the invention of a talking watch, which will achieve the utmost facility and dispatch in the communication of ideas by a graduated adjustment of ticks, to be represented in writing by a corresponding arrangement of dots.[7]

George Eliot's own use of dialect was most thorough in *Adam Bede,* rather less so in *The Mill on the Floss.* In the latter novel there is a colloquialism often shared by the characters and the narrator, though the narrator is clearly the more highly educated. The narrator speaks as a natural historian, an observer and analyst of individual and social life. In this persona George Eliot draws strikingly on the language of natural growth, animal husbandry, and animal behavior to describe human actions. Mrs. Tulliver is like "a patriarchal goldfish" swimming unthinkingly against the "resisting medium" of the glass goldfish bowl (134). She is an "amiable hen" in her attempts to put matters right between her husband and Mr. Wakem (332). The strained relations between Wakem and Tulliver are likened to those between a pike and a roach (338). Though this last example is rather facetious, the explanatory function it performs would be immediately clear to most of the characters in the novel, accustomed as they are to the habits of many animals and plants. The Tullivers and Dodsons speak colorfully and metaphorically as a natural concomitant of their social and agrarian environment.

George Eliot recognized this characteristic of *The Mill on the Floss* when she replied sympathetically to her Swiss friend (and possible model for Philip Wakem) François D'Albert-Durade, who was engaged on the French translation of the novel in 1861:

> I can well imagine that you find "The Mill" more difficult to render than "Adam." But would it be inadmissible to represent in French, at least in some degree, those "intermédiaires entre le style commun et le style élégant" to which you refer? It seems to me that I have discerned such shades very strikingly rendered in Balzac, and occasionally in George Sand. Balzac, I think, dares to be thoroughly colloquial, in spite of French straitlacing. Even in English this daring is far from being general. The writers who dare to be thoroughly familiar are Shakespeare, Fielding, Scott (where he is expressing the popular life with which he is familiar), and indeed every other writer of fiction of the first class. Even in his loftiest tragedies—in Hamlet, for example—Shakespeare is intensely colloquial.[8]

Here George Eliot ranges herself with those writers, English and French, whom she most admired. And it may be that she singles out one of Shakespeare's tragedies for comparison in the consciousness that her own novel represented an attempt to marry the pastoral, realist, and colloquial with grand tragedy.

True to her creed of "Dutch realism" as practiced in *Adam Bede,* she observes in *The Mill on the Floss* that millers and small farmers do not speak in standard English, and it would be a falsehood to render them doing so. Interestingly, though, the children of the Tulliver and Dodson generation do learn to speak standard English as they grow up. This is one of the many examples by means of which George Eliot indicates the social changes taking place during the time spanned by the novel. Tom and Maggie, though living too early to benefit from the universal education laws of the years after 1870, and though enduring a schooling less than perfect for their needs, do receive more than the rudimentary instruction one assumes their parents to have enjoyed. Ironically, while George Eliot's scrupulous observation of this particular form of social change is a part of her attempt at realism, it is one of the factors combining to make the last third of the novel, in which we see less of the older residents of St. Ogg's and more of the younger ones, seem a different kind of novel from the first two thirds.

The opening of Book 1, chapter 2, provides us with an excellent example of the dense and multiple effects that George Eliot achieves by means of a suggestion of local dialect:

> "What I want, you know," said Mr. Tulliver, "what I want is to give Tom a good eddication: an eddication as'll be a bread to him. That was what I was thinking on when I gave notice for him to leave th'Academy at Ladyday. I mean to put him to a downright good school at Midsummer. The two years at th'Academy 'ud ha' done well enough, if I'd meant to make a miller and farmer of him, for he's had a fine sight more schoolin' nor *I* ever got: all the learnin' *my* father ever paid for was for a bit o' birch at one end and the alphabet at th'other. But I should like Tom to be a bit of a scholard, so as he might be up to the tricks o' these fellows as talk fine and write wi' a flourish. It 'ud be a help to me wi' these law-suits and arbitrations and things. I wouldn't make a downright lawyer o' the lad—I should be sorry for him to be a raskill—but a sort o' engineer, or a surveyor, or an auctioneer and vallyer, like Riley, or one o' them smartish businesses as are all profits and no outlay, only for a big watch-chain and a high stool. They're

pretty nigh all one, and they're not far off being even wi' the law, *I* believe; for Riley looks Lawyer Wakem i' the face as hard as one cat looks at another. *He's* none frighted at him." (56)

First, Mr. Tulliver's speech is a living thing; it sounds genuine. There is no outlandish or unrecognizable vocabulary; George Eliot simply renders provincial speech by an accent, a rhythm, and a slight deviation from normal grammar. Then the topic of conversation is, appropriately, education and the proud, independent miller's "natural" desire that his son should have advantages he himself never enjoyed. Moreover, Mr. Tulliver's habit of mind is portrayed—he is litigious, having both a suspicion of and a fascination with the law and lawyers. George Eliot had noted in her review of W. H. von Riehl's books on German history that peasants and farmers are notoriously addicted to resorting to lawsuits over land disputes: "The farmer's lawsuit is his point of honour; and he will carry it through, though he knows from the very first day that he shall get nothing by it."[9] Mr. Tulliver's "going to law," and particularly his dealings with Mr. Wakem, will lead to his downfall and sow the seeds of future unhappiness for his children. Thus not only is a social tone set in this paragraph, but the plot is well begun in as natural an expository style as one could wish for. George Eliot herself, as narrator, will intervene to comment as the novel goes on, but she begins her story by letting her character himself broach the topics of future interest to himself and his fellow creations.

People, in *The Mill on the Floss,* reveal their complex natures through their habits of speech. In a general way, the Dodson sisters display their obsession with "kin" and domesticity by their constant talk of small, local matters: china, hats, medicines, the optimum time to take meals, the making of butter. Their loving and fanatical concentration on these family details extends naturally and, importantly for the plot, to niggardly care in money matters and decided views on when to lend and when to refuse. Yet, so subtle is George Eliot's grasp of the mixed motives and odd mental twists that lie behind action that she can show Mrs. Glegg and the others acting harshly toward Mr. Tulliver when he faces financial ruin—why throw good money after bad?—and yet allow the same Mrs. Glegg to surprise us by showing a generous faith in Maggie after the scandal with Stephen. George Eliot makes us see that though these actions and attitudes may seem incompatible, they stem from the same mental root. In Mrs. Glegg's view Mr. Tulliver has brought ruin on himself, despite advice from herself and the other aunts and uncles; moreover, he is not quite kin, merely kin-in-law. Maggie, on the other hand, has Dodson blood in her as well as Tulliver, and "if you were not to stand by your 'kin' as long as there was a shred of honour attributable to them, pray what were you to stand by?" As George Eliot comments: "The circumstances were unprecedented in Mrs. Glegg's experience—nothing of that kind had happened among the Dodsons before; but it was a case in which her hereditary rectitude and personal strength of character found a common channel along with her fundamental ideas of clanship, as they did in her lifelong regard to equity in money matters" (629).

Most interesting of all, in this respect, is the brilliant portrayal of Mr. Tulliver's mental confusion. Thinking himself shrewd and worldly-wise because he is a good miller and suspicious of others' intentions, he makes a series of practical mistakes that together bring about his personal tragedy. Generosity to his sister combines with irascibility at the interference of his in-laws, with whom he has become financially involved, to make him act hastily while thinking himself amazingly prudent. As George Eliot puts it in a telling metaphor: "Mr. Tulliver, when under the influence of a strong feeling, had a promptitude in action that may seem inconsistent with that painful sense of the complicated puzzling nature of human affairs under which his more dispassionate deliberations were conducted; but it is really not improbable that there was a direct relation between these apparently contradictory phenomena, since I have observed that for getting a strong impression that a skein is tangled, there is nothing like snatching hastily at a single thread" (135). But, as with Aunt Glegg, George Eliot quite as often lets Mr. Tulliver illustrate his nature by the language he uses as she applies her own analytical descriptions to him. Referring to Maggie's cleverness and Tom's relative dullness, he says:

> "It's a pity but what she'd been the lad—she'd ha' been a match for the lawyers, *she* would. It's the wonderful'st thing"—here he lowered his

voice—"as I picked the mother because she wasn't o'er cute—bein' a
good-looking woman too, an' come of a rare family for managing—
but I picked her from her sisters o' purpose 'cause she was a bit weak,
like; for I wasn't a-goin' to be told the rights o' things by my own fire-
side. But, you see, when a man's got brains himself, there's no knowing
where they'll run to; an' a pleasant sort o' soft woman may go on
breeding you stupid lads and 'cute wenches, till it's like as if the world
was turned topsy-turvy. It's an uncommon puzzlin' thing." (68–69)

Here is the familiar obsession with the enviable yet not-to-be-
trusted cleverness of lawyers, the miller's pride in his own acuteness in
choosing a stupid wife as a natural foil to his imagined intelligence, and
the characteristic lapse into puzzlement at the way things turn out. "This
world's been too many for me" becomes his pathetic refrain as his fortunes sink ever lower.

Mr. Tulliver also, we should note, uses in this speech the language of
natural selection. He does so innocently, as it were (i.e., without having
read Darwin), and naturally for a countryman. But in using this language
to describe his relationship with his wife, he is in harmony with a pervasive authorial vocabulary, very much aware of Darwinism. George Eliot
says of Mr. Tulliver's very habits of speech that they have a tendency toward causticity "which had remained in rather an embryonic or inarticu-
late condition" (132).[10] In considering the realism, or naturalism, of the
speech and the psychological motivation observed in *The Mill on the
Floss*, we must take into account the importance of George Eliot's
knowledge of, and adherence to, the theory and language of evolution.

Chapter 5

Natural History

George Eliot began writing *The Mill on the Floss* in January 1859. Darwin's great work, the full title of which is *On the Origin of Species by Means of Natural Selection; or the Preservation of Favoured Races in the Struggle for Life,* appeared in November 1859, when she was nearing the end of her novel. Since George Eliot's use of the language of natural science to describe the progress of her characters, psychologically and socially, occurs predominantly in the first half of her book, written before Darwin's work was published, we must be careful not to talk of a direct influence of Darwin on her work.

As with so many famous "discoveries," Darwin's book represented more a striking and climactic formulation of facts and theories already much aired by naturalists and geologists (e.g., Lamarck, Sir Charles Lyell, and Alfred Russel Wallace, to all of whom Darwin pays generous tribute in his introduction) than a sudden emergence of new ideas. George Eliot, thanks to her wide reading and her relationship with Lewes, whose main interest since writing his biography of Goethe had been scientific, was well versed in the arguments and language of natural history.

That *The Mill on the Floss* in particular should be so full of scientific language is due partly, no doubt, to her having spent all her holidays since

1856 accompanying Lewes on his rambles along the coasts of England and Wales in search of marine life to study and dissect. Lewes published a set of lively essays on the subject in *Blackwood's Magazine* during 1856 and 1857, later collecting them in a book entitled *Sea-Side Studies at Ilfracombe, Tenby, the Scilly Isles and Jersey* (1858). So *au fait* was George Eliot with the terms of the debate among scientists about the development theory and the variation as opposed to fixity of species that when Darwin's long-awaited work appeared, she was inclined to underrate its importance. "We are reading Darwin's Book on Species, just come out, after long expectation," she wrote to Charles Bray on 25 November 1859. "It is an elaborate exposition of the evidence in favour of the Development Theory, and so, makes an epoch."[1] But to another friend she confided that she thought the book "ill-written and sadly wanting in illustrative facts." Moreover, she felt that "the Development theory and all explanations of processes by which things came to be, produce a feeble impression compared with the mystery that lies under the processes."[2] This muted estimate of Darwin's work is probably to be explained both by her real familiarity with his material and propositions and by some jealous pride in Lewes's achievements in the same field. A reading of *Sea-Side Studies* shows that Lewes was indeed a "Darwinist" before Darwin published his findings, so George Eliot's lack of excitement at *The Origin of Species* has its explanation. On the other hand, only the most partial observer, on reading the two works, could seek to deny Darwin the status he has been accorded in the history of ideas. To him belongs the distinction of having discovered the mechanism of natural selection to explain the development of species, and his work is a fine blend of patient observation and example with speculative theory. Lewes made no claim to have discovered new laws. His essays were avowedly a lively popularizing of natural science, in which the many examples are used to interest and amuse the reader rather than engage his understanding of, or assent to, a theory. The full titles of the two works alert us to their difference in scope and tone.

What Darwin and Lewes share is subject matter and a tendency to interpret it without reference to divine creation of species. Indeed, in his *Studies in Animal Life* (1861–62) Lewes defended Darwin's belief that species were variable, not fixed, against his many orthodox critics. When we talk of George Eliot's Darwinian vocabulary and outlook in *The Mill on the Floss,* we take our sanction for doing so from the agreement between George Eliot, Darwin, and Lewes and from her firsthand knowledge of the state of scientific experiment and debate in 1859.

George Eliot's use of scientific language is analogical. In *The Mill on the Floss* natural science provides her with a rich fund of metaphors to describe the motives and actions of her characters. Mr. Stelling, the clergyman fixed on by Mr. Tulliver to teach Tom, tries to force the classics into Tom's ill-equipped head. George Eliot finds an example from her recent reading to express the absurdity of this course of action, while recognizing how "natural" it is for Mr. Stelling to follow it:

> Mr. Broderip's amiable beaver, as that charming naturalist tells us, busied himself as earnestly in constructing a dam, in a room up three pairs of stairs in London, as if he had been laying his foundation in a stream or lake in Upper Canada. It was "Binny's" function to build: the absence of water or of possible progeny was an accident for which he was not accountable. With the same unerring instinct Mr. Stelling set to work at his natural method of instilling the Eton Grammar and Euclid into the mind of Tom Tulliver. This, he considered, was the only basis of solid instruction: all other means of education were mere charlatanism, and could produce nothing better than smatterers. (206–7)[3]

Still on the topic of Tom's unfortunate education, the author asks: "Besides, how should Mr. Stelling be expected to know that education was a delicate and difficult business? any more than an animal endowed with a power of boring a hole through rock should be expected to have wide views of excavation. Mr. Stelling's faculties had been early trained to boring in a strait [*sic*] line, and he had no faculty to spare" (241). Such examples of the illustrative use of scientific observation abound in the novel.

But George Eliot uses this language in a way that is literal as well as metaphorical. The development theory with which she was so familiar in 1859 entails a belief in the interrelatedness, as well as differentiation, of species. Darwin and others put the case against the creation of different species and for the development of species over time from a very few original types by means of inheritance, variation, and adaptation to circumstances. In *The Origin of Species* he expressed his belief in the organic nature of all species (including, by implication, the human species):

> It is a truly wonderful fact—the wonder of which we are apt to over
> look from familiarity—that all animals and all plants throughout all
> time and space should be related to each other in group subordinate to
> group, in the manner which we everywhere behold—namely, varieties
> of the same species most closely related together, species of the same
> genus less closely and unequally related together, forming sections and
> sub-genera, species of distinct genera much less closely related, and
> genera related in different degrees, forming sub-families, families, or
> ders, sub-classes, and classes. The several subordinate groups in any
> class cannot be ranked in a single file, but seem rather to be clustered
> round points, and these round other points, and so on in almost end
> less cycles. On the view that each species has been independently cre
> ated, I can see no explanation of this great fact in the classification of
> all organic beings; but, to the best of my judgment, it is explained
> through inheritance and the complex action of natural selection, en
> tailing extinction and divergence of character.[4]

George Eliot wholeheartedly embraced this view of all life as interrelated. Its implications for the understanding of human behavior were
important and far-reaching. Mr. Stelling, in her descriptions, is "like" a
beaver and a marine animal boring through rock because he shares with
them a tendency to act on instinct and only a partial ability to adapt to
prevailing circumstances. To study animal or plant life is to learn about
human life, too. As Lewes put it, "all the forms and facts of Nature" are
"manifestations of the Universal Life."[5] And George Eliot's persistent use
of animal and plant terminology in her analysis of human nature combines the literary function of giving imaginative color to her subject with
the philosophical function of illustrating general human truths.

There is, as a result of her acceptance of the close kinship between
human and animal types, a boldness about *The Mill on the Floss* compared to most contemporary novels. Her generally deferential publisher, John Blackwood, objected to the description of Mrs. Tulliver as
"the stout lymphatic woman" (282), and to that of Aunt Moss as "a

patient, loosely-hung, child-producing woman" (139), on the grounds that "some might take exception" to them.[6] George Eliot accepted his mild criticism, and changed the passages to include the more innocuous phrases, "the stout blond woman" and "a patient, prolific, loving-hearted woman," respectively.[7] However, much remained to raise the eyebrows of protected readers and critics, though it is a tribute to George Eliot's achievement that even while they objected, critics echoed Blackwood's admiration of her genius. Blackwood reported J. T. Delane, editor of the *Times,* as saying in this connection, "God it is a wonderful book. It is no use arguing about it."[8]

As we have seen, George Eliot lets her Dodsons and Tullivers, farmers and millers, talk directly and "naturally" in terms of livestock when discussing their own family life. When Mr. Tulliver wants to express his opinion that Maggie is more intelligent than Tom and his fear that she will somehow come to grief as a result, he resorts to the vocabulary of the farmer:

> "It seems a bit of a pity, though," said Mr. Tulliver, "as the lad should take after the mother's side istead o' the little wench. That's the worst on't wi' the crossing o' breeds: you can never justly calkilate what'll come on't. The little un takes after my side, now: she's twice as 'cute as Tom. Too 'cute for a woman, I'm afraid," continued Mr. Tulliver, turning his head dubiously first on one side and then on the other. "It's no mischief much while she's a little un, but an over 'cute woman's no better nor a long-tailed sheep—she'll fetch none the bigger price for that." (59–60)

In such a passage George Eliot achieves several aims at once. First, in accordance with her principle of realism, she represents how a country miller who keeps farm animals would really illustrate his meaning from his own near experience. The remark is at the same time psychologically in keeping with Mr. Tulliver's weakness for self-congratulation and over-estimation of his own intelligence. On a wider front, George Eliot lets him represent in his speech the prevailing notion of society that boys should be educated more seriously than girls in preparation for the active lives they are to lead. Intelligence in a girl is a misfortune, being a hindrance to her chances in the marriage market. This is an important theme in the novel and one to which I return in chapter 10. Then, too, the author stands behind Mr. Tulliver, making, through him, the point that human nature, like animal nature, is a volatile mixture of the predictable—that offspring will inherit characteristics from both parents—and the unpredictable—the impossibility of knowing precisely which characteristics will predominate in any given case. Finally, mindful that she is writing a novel rather than an illustrative history of the development of species, she lets Mr. Tulliver predict in his own way an unhappy future for Maggie, one the specific plot of *The Mill on the Floss* will tragically fulfill.

Natural history so thoroughly informs the writing of *The Mill on the Floss* that it contributes to both the comedy and the tragedy of the book. The portrayal of the Dodson aunts, whom George Eliot's contemporary critics so loved to hate, is rooted in the observation of family likeness with individual variations. George Eliot quite brilliantly illustrates the strengths and weaknesses of family relations by means of Darwinian language, at the same time dropping prophetic hints at plot level. As we have seen, the Dodson trait of putting "kin" above other folks issues later in Aunt Glegg's standing by Maggie in her disgrace. Another of the aunts, Aunt Pullet, is the "channel of fatality" by which Tom finds out that Maggie is secretly meeting Philip Wakem. With her Dodson obsession with ill health and her propensity to exaggerate, she brings Philip into a general conversation among the family about height and beauty:

> "Ah, it's poor talking about littleness and bigness,—anybody might think it's a mercy they're straight," said aunt Pullet. "There's that mismade son o' Lawyer Wakem's—I saw him at church today. Dear, dear! to think o' the property he's like to have. And they say he's very queer and unked—doesn't like much company. I shouldn't wonder if he goes out of his mind, for we never come along the road but he's a-scrambling out o' the trees and brambles at the Red Deeps."
> This wide statement, by which Mrs. Pullet represented the fact that she had twice seen Philip at the spot indicated, produced an effect on Maggie which was all the stronger because Tom sate [*sic*] opposite her, and she was intensely anxious to look indifferent. (441)

Where Darwin narrates the "plot" of natural history in a largely cheerful, neutral way, observing how over time some species and some individuals belonging to a species succeed in adapting and varying in the ways necessary for survival, while others fail, George Eliot narrates her plot on a smaller sample and a smaller time scale, a fact that entails our becoming engaged with the fates, comic and tragic, of her people.[9] Thus Mrs. Tulliver, the feeblest of the sisters, and chosen for that reason by Mr. Tulliver, as we have seen, is still enough of a Dodson to insist on having her way in certain areas of domestic life. George Eliot writes of the family characteristics in such a way that she places each individual member while at the same time indicating what we might call, in keeping with our topic, the life of the tribe and the social pecking order of St. Ogg's, an order in which the Dodsons rank slightly higher than the Tullivers:

> Few wives were more submissive than Mrs. Tulliver on all points unconnected with her family relations; but she had been a Miss Dodson, and the Dodsons were a very respectable family indeed—as much looked up to as any in their own parish or the next to it. The Miss Dodsons had always been thought to hold up their heads very high, and no one was surprised the two eldest had married so well—not at an early age, for that was not the practice of the Dodson family. There were particular ways of doing everything in that family: particular ways of bleaching the linen, of making the cowslip wine, curing the hams and keeping the bottled gooseberries, so that no daughter of that house could be indifferent to the privilege of having been born a Dodson, rather than a Gibson or a Watson.... A female Dodson, when in "strange houses," always ate dry bread with her tea and declined any sort of preserves, having no confidence in the butter and thinking that the preserves had probably begun to ferment from want of due sugar and boiling. (96–97)

Having thus established the family resemblances, George Eliot observes that "there were some Dodsons less like the family than others—that was admitted—but in so far as they were 'kin,' they were of necessity better than those who were 'no kin.' And it is remarkable that while no individual Dodson was satisfied with any other individual Dodson, each was satisfied, not only with him or herself, but with the Dodsons collectively." (97). Thus Mrs. Tulliver is "a thorough Dodson, though a mild one," enjoying, paradoxically yet in terms of hereditary and social considerations quite explicably, a feeling of superiority toward her opinionated husband: "she was thankful to have been a Dodson, and to have one child who took after her own family, at least in his features and complexion, in liking salt, and in eating beans, which a Tulliver never did" (97).

The comic mode in which George Eliot consistently treats the "Dodson sisterhood," as Blackwood called them, has perhaps one disadvantage. We are meant to laugh at them with their grotesquely old-fashioned dress and their bickering over minutiae. George Eliot is almost Fieldingesque in her mock-dramatic introduction of them in a chapter entitled "Enter the Aunts and Uncles." Here Mrs. Glegg's antediluvian attire is minutely described:

> Mrs. Glegg chose to wear her bonnet in the house to-day—untied and tilted slightly, of course—a frequent practice of hers when she was on a visit and happened to be in a severe humour: she didn't know what draughts there might be in strange houses. For the same reason she wore a small sable tippet which reached just to her shoulders and was very far from meeting across her well-formed chest, while her long neck was protected by a *chevaux-de-frise* of miscellaneous frilling. One would need to be learned in the fashions of those times to know how far in the rear of them Mrs. Glegg's slate-coloured silk gown must have been, but from certain constellations of small yellow spots upon it, and a mouldy odour about it suggestive of a damp clothes-chest, it was probable that it belonged to a stratum of garments just old enough to have come recently into wear. (109)

This is as good an example of satirical writing as one can find in the annals of English comic fiction, from Fielding to Thackeray, but notably the language also includes the vocabulary of science. Mrs. Glegg's wardrobe, with its strata of garments, is a geologist's dream. Mrs. Pullet, the most crudely drawn of the sisters, also represents a particular stage in the history of dress, in this case mourning dress:

From the sorrow of a Hottentot to that of a woman in large buckram sleeves, with several bracelets on each arm, an architectural bonnet and delicate ribbon-strings—what a long series of gradations! In the enlightened child of civilisation the abandonment characteristic of grief is checked and varied in the subtlest manner, so as to present an interesting problem to the analytic mind. If, with a crushed heart and eyes half-blinded by the mist of tears, she were to walk with a too devious step through a doorplace, she might crush her buckram sleeves too, and the deep consciousness of this possibility produces a composition of forces by which she takes a line that just clears the doorpost. (111–12)

The combination in these and other passages of, on the one hand, high but rather bitter hilarity at the Dodsons' expense and, on the other, natural historical observation may confuse the reader. It may sometimes seem that the scientific observation, which is part of the mode of seeing these characters, is itself something comic. This is, of course, not the case. Comic as the aunts are, George Eliot means them to illustrate general laws of human behavior. In an important, if rather opaque, address to the reader in the first chapter of Book 4, she tackles the subject of the narrowness of the Dodson view of life. As Darwin calls to his aid the findings of geology to illustrate the generation of plants and animals, so also does George Eliot in her illustrated social history of the inhabitants of St. Ogg's. Comparing them to the ugly "skeletons of villages" on the banks of the Rhône, she observes: "I have a cruel conviction that the lives these ruins are the traces of were part of a gross sum of obscure vitality, that will be swept into the same oblivion with the generations of ants and beavers" (362).

Perhaps, she continues, readers feel similarly oppressed by the sordid, narrow life of "these emmet-like Dodsons and Tullivers":

I share with you this sense of oppressive narrowness; but it is necessary that we should feel it, if we care to understand how it acted on the lives of Tom and Maggie—how it has acted on young natures in many generations, that in the onward tendency of human things have risen above the mental level of the generation before them, to which they have been nevertheless tied by the strongest fibres of their hearts. (363)

Narrow and provincial as the Dodson-Tulliver life is, it illustrates the onward movement of generations as much as the life of any famous martyr. There is an indissoluble connection between the great and the humble. "In natural science," the author concludes, "there is nothing petty to the mind that has a large vision of relations, and to which every single object suggests a vast sum of conditions. It is surely the same with the observation of human life" (363).

This plea to take proper account of seemingly petty phenomena recalls Lewes's similar defense of natural science at the end of *Sea-Side Studies:*

> Unreflecting minds often deem it a trivial occupation for serious men to devote themselves with patience to the study of anatomical details, and the scrutiny of facts which seem to have no practical bearing on the great affairs of life. These details, like all other facts of Nature, may, indeed, be studied in a trivial spirit, uninspired by a loftier aim; but under their lowest aspect they have still the inalienable value attendant upon all truth; and under their highest aspect they teach us something of a noble wisdom which profoundly affects the practical affairs of life, by affecting the direction and the temper of our thoughts.[10]

George Eliot's use of the optimistic phrase "the onward tendency of human things" is important. Maggie and Tom are better educated than their parents (and speak standard English to prove it), and both consequently rise above their parents in the social scale. This is a statement of George Eliot's (albeit qualified) belief in progress. We may compare it with Darwin's similarly optimistic claim in the conclusion to *The Origin of Species:* "And as natural selection works solely by and for the good of each being, all corporeal and mental endowments will tend to progress towards perfection."[11] But if an optimistic note is sounded to illustrate a general perception, the particular case may often be an unhappy one. Darwin, whose task is to take the large view, can discuss with equanimity the "general law, leading to the advancement of all organic beings, namely, multiply, vary, let the strongest live and the weakest die."[12] The particular story that George Eliot finds herself telling is a pessimistic one, in which husbands and wives, brothers and sisters, millers and lawyers, thwart one another's interests, not always intentionally, and several individuals do not survive in the battle for existence.

Here her decision to write a tragic novel comes into play. As in nature there are happy endings for some, so in the novel some characters—though emphatically not the central ones—flourish. Socially and economically, the Deane and Pullet branches of the family thrive, while the Tullivers decline. The family history is metonymic of a general social trend during the early nineteenth century: the movement of local wealth and position from inherited land and old-fashioned pursuits, such as Tulliver's mill, to trade and partnerships based not solely on inheritance, as represented by the firm of Guest & Co. and Uncle Deane's relation to it. In the course of describing a domestic scene among the aunts, uncles, and cousins, the narrator discusses the provenance of a silver snuff box:

> Mr. Deane's box had been given him by the superior partners in the firm to which he belonged, at the same time that they gave him a share in the business in acknowledgement of his valuable services as manager. No man was thought more highly of in St. Ogg's than Mr. Deane, and some persons were even of opinion that Miss Susan Dodson, who was held to have made the worst match of all the Dodson sisters, might one day ride in a better carriage and live in a better house even than her sister Pullet. There was no knowing where a man would stop, who had got his foot into a great mill-owning, ship-owning business like that of Guest & Co. with a banking concern attached. (119)

Later, in chapter 3 of Book 3 ("The Downfall"), a painful comparison is invoked. Mr. Tulliver is threatened with bankruptcy; a family council is held; Mrs. Deane arrives in "a handsome new gig with the head to it and the livery servant driving it." As in classical tragedy the wheel of fortune turns, depositing some at the bottom and raising others high, so in the history of social relations there are those who thrive under new conditions and those who go under: "Mr. Deane had been advancing in the world as rapidly as Mr. Tulliver had been going down in it" (286).

Critics took George Eliot to task for her pessimistic view of family and group life as a battle; and hers was indeed a melancholy vision. Thus Tom and Maggie are unhappy, for reasons partly inherent in their particular combination of inherited family traits and partly resulting from what George Eliot calls "external fact." "No wonder," she says of Maggie's probable future, "when there is this contrast between the outward and the inward, that painful collisions come of it." In the manuscript there follows an illustration omitted from the first edition: "A girl of no startling appearance, and who will never be a Sappho or a Madame Roland or anything else that the world takes wide note of, may still hold forces within her as the living plant-seed does, which will make a way for themselves, often in a shattering, violent manner" (320).[13]

In a quite unique and startling way George Eliot here combines the traditional literary and philosophical principle of tragedy from Sophocles to Shakespeare and beyond—the combination of individual weakness in the hero or heroine and a set of unfortunate external circumstances—with a pessimistic interpretation of the progress and extinction of individual seeds, embryos, and even species in the natural world. The overwhelming impression one has after reading *The Mill on the Floss* is that life is a largely tragic affair. For while in nature the survival of the fittest is a morally neutral doctrine, the fittest being simply that, in human society the survivors may not always be, morally speaking, those most deserving to survive. In these cases, tragedy is invoked. The telling of *The Mill on the Floss* moves with ease between the vocabulary of natural history and that of Greek tragedy. As the last sentence of Book 1 has it with reference to Mr. Tulliver's entanglements: "Mr. Tulliver had a destiny as well as Oedipus, and in this case he might plead, like Oedipus, that his deed was inflicted on him rather than committed by him" (198).

Chapter 6

Tragedy

Though most of George Eliot's works contain elements of tragedy, *The Mill on the Floss* is the only truly tragic novel she wrote; that is, it is the only one in which the protagonists suffer and die, leaving behind a sense of waste. Paradoxically, as with Greek and Shakespearean tragedy, there is also a sense of fulfillment, of death as a high release from troubled lives. Thus, at the end of the novel the great flood sweeps Maggie and Tom to their death in a last embrace, happy together in a way that had proved impossible while they lived. But the question of exactly where the tragedy lies is a complex one. It is not even immediately clear who the tragic protagonists are.

That Maggie is the heroine is, of course, not in doubt. She is lovingly (occasionally too much so) handled by the narrator, and the title of the novel was to have been, until Blackwood suggested a new one at George Eliot's request, "Sister Maggie."[1] But who is the hero? Many Victorian critics thought it was meant to be Stephen Guest, though they rightly found him very unsatisfactory in the role, as we have seen. It is certainly Maggie's quasi-elopement with Stephen that forms the moral crisis of the book, ruining once and for all the happiness of Maggie, Stephen, Philip, Lucy Deane, and Tom. But the dramatic catastrophe does not follow of necessity from the moral one, and its embodiment, the flood, engulfs not Maggie and Stephen but Maggie and Tom. There is therefore a division of interest in the last chapters of the novel that is confusing and that has led many readers to complain. One contemporary critic thought that George Eliot did not know "how to bring her story to a natural end"; a representative modern critic has written of the "quite artificial resolution" of the tragedy.[2] We know that George Eliot intended the novel to be tragic from the beginning, and that she envisaged a flood for the climax, studying "cases of inundation" in the *Annual Register* as early as January 1859.[3] The problem of division of interest stems in part from the structure of the novel, both this novel in particular and the genre itself.

Where tragic drama combines narrative with compression, having a pattern of exposition, climax or catastrophe, and return to stability, the novel is a more completely narrative form. It allows for more than one main plot and one subplot, it can accommodate many more characters, and because of its greater length it is generally less symbolic, less intense, less highly patterned than drama. Add to this the insistence of the narrator of this particular novel that he is an observer of a natural history of provincial life, studying the gradual evolution of a society, St. Ogg's, within a time scale not as large, certainly, as that required for the variation of plant and animal species, but large enough to include a history of St. Ogg's going back to Roman times and beyond into ancient legend:

> It is one of those old, old towns, which impress one as a continuation and outgrowth of nature as much as the nests of the bower birds or the winding galleries of the white ants: a town which carries the traces of its long growth and history, like a millennial tree, and has sprung up and developed in the same spot between the river and the low hill from the time when the Roman legions turned their backs on it from the camp on the hill-side, and the long-haired sea-kings came up the river and looked with fierce, eager eyes at the fatness of the land. . . .
>
> But older even than this old Hall is perhaps the bit of wall now built into the belfry of the parish church and said to be a remnant of the original chapel dedicated to St. Ogg, the patron saint of this ancient town, of whose history I possess several manuscript versions. (181–82)[4]

This tendency to extend the scope of the narrative in a way unusual even in Victorian novels aligns *The Mill on the Floss* more to epic than to drama. As George Eliot acknowledged, she may have overdone the "epic breadth" of the first two thirds of the novel, thus causing "a want of proportionate fullness" in the treatment of the crisis in the last third.[5]

Any tragic novel must contain a collision between two opposite urges: the urge to brevity, climax, the working out of an individual's fate, and the urge to extension, ordinariness, and pluralism. George Eliot, in undertaking to combine a natural historical plot and a tragic one, runs a heightened risk of failing to reconcile the conflict. Nevertheless, as we shall see in chapter 8, she took great care to prepare for the tragic outcome through symbolism, dream, legend, and tight plotting.

Tragic drama, with the notable and controversial exception of Shakespeare's *Antony and Cleopatra,* usually embodies the downfall of one individual, not two. The tragic death of the hero follows directly and logically from the climax: Oedipus' discovery of his relations with his mother and father, Lear's finding Cordelia dead in her cell. Maggie's death, as we have seen, is not connected plotwise to the catastrophe, though it may well be that it is for the author a psychologically necessary solution to her heroine's problem. Maggie cannot live with her mistake. She must die, and for her death to be fully tragic it must include Tom. For it is clear that Tom is the tragic hero of the novel; of all Maggie's loving relationships—with Philip, Tom, and Stephen—that with Tom is the most powerful. The working title George Eliot used, "Sister Maggie," illustrates the point. So also does another title favored by George Eliot and Lewes until Blackwood suggested the neutral, natural-historical *Mill on the Floss:* "The House of Tulliver, or, Life on the Floss."[6] There is an unmistakable echo of Greek tragedy here: Oedipus belonged to the doomed house of Atreus, against whom the gods, or fate, had a grudge which took generations to work through to its end. We have seen that the narrator of *The Mill on the Floss* compares Mr. Tulliver's fate to that of Oedipus. In both cases the tragedy is a family one. (This helps to explain why we cannot take Stephen seriously as a tragic hero: he does not figure in the central drama of the book.)

George Eliot's reading and her personal experience both told her that the strongest ties are family ones; it follows that the deepest disappointments occur within family relationships too. Her own father almost threw her out of the house when she stopped going to church;[7] her brother, Isaac, spoke and wrote no word to her from the time he heard, in 1857, of her liaison with Lewes to the moment she told him of her legal marriage to John Cross, six months before her death, in 1880. In *Adam Bede* the narrator describes the family tie as tragic: "Family likeness has often a deep sadness in it. Nature, that great tragic dramatist, knits us together by bone and muscle, and divides us by the subtler web of our brains; blends yearning and repulsion; and ties us by our heartstrings to the beings that jar us at every movement."[8] George Eliot's reading of natural history confirmed the pessimistic view she already took of family life: the struggle for survival includes a trampling on those nearest us.

Before dealing with the tragedy of Maggie's relationship with Tom, I should like to look at the less problematic, but connected, tragedy that befalls their father. The downfall and death of Mr. Tulliver are as skillfully plotted as those of Oedipus. They occur as a result of a fateful combination of circumstances. His pride, stubbornness, and penchant for lawsuits lead him into financial difficulties that can, as it happens, only be eased by his becoming indebted to Wakem, the lawyer whom he half-irrationally blames for his predicament. This further chafes his independent spirit. The more he becomes beholden to his "enemy," the more gloomy and unpredictable he becomes. His death is brought on by overexcitement after he has thrashed Wakem, ironically at a time when Tom has managed to save enough money to pay off his father's creditors and ease his shame at being dependent on others. The narrator comments on the family unhappiness: "Apparently the mingled thread in the web of their life was so curiously twisted together that there could be no joy without a sorrow coming close upon it" (462).

In a tragicomic foretaste of Maggie's and Tom's constant thwarting of each other's purposes, Mrs. Tulliver is prominent in the undoing of her difficult husband. Early on she is the partial means of hastening his financial entanglement with Wakem by reminding him at an unwelcome moment of his having previously borrowed from her sister Mrs. Glegg. A family quarrel over Tom's education has caused a coolness with Mrs. Glegg and a threat that she will recall her £500. In attempting to avoid this, Mrs. Tulliver merely ensures its occurrence. A biological metaphor describes the process by which Mrs. Tulliver rubs her irascible mate up the wrong way:

> Mrs. Tulliver had lived thirteen years with her husband, yet she retained in all the freshness of her early married life a facility of saying things which drove him in the opposite direction to the one she desired. Some minds are wonderful for keeping their bloom in this way, as a patriarchal goldfish apparently retains to the last its youthful illusion that it can swim in a straight line beyond the encircling glass. Mrs. Tulliver was an amiable fish of this kind, and after running her head against the same resisting medium for thirteen years would go at it again to-day with undulled alacrity. (134)

Mrs. Tulliver thus hastens the "catastrophe" by which proud Mr. Tulliver pays back Mrs. Glegg unnecessarily, a proceeding that obliges him to encumber himself with a £500 debt elsewhere. Tragic irony requires that his possibilities for action be limited:

> Mr. Tulliver's prompt procedure entailed on him further promptitude in finding the convenient person who was desirous of lending five hundred pounds on bond. "It must be no client of Wakem's," he said to himself; and yet at the end of a fortnight it turned out to the contrary; not because Mr. Tulliver's will was feeble, but because external fact was stronger. Wakem's client was the only convenient person to be found. Mr. Tulliver had a destiny as well as Oedipus, and in this case he might plead, like Oedipus, that his deed was inflicted on him rather than committed by him. (198)

Natural history again provides the language for Mrs. Tulliver's further disastrous effort to improve matters. Mr. Tulliver, now ill and obliged to sell the mill to settle his debts, has the hope that his brother-in-law Mr. Deane will buy it on behalf of Guest & Co., keeping Mr. Tulliver on as manager. Much as this dependent situation goes against the grain with Mr. Tulliver, it is preferable to another possibility, namely, that

Wakem will buy it. Mrs. Tulliver sets out to avert this latter possibility, with the melancholy effect of turning it into a certainty. "Imagine a truly respectable and amiable hen," says the narrator, "by some portentous anomaly, taking to reflection and inventing combinations by which she might prevail on Hodge not to wring her neck or send her and her chicks to market: the result could hardly be other than much cackling and fluttering" (332). The irony of speech and event with which we are familiar in Greek tragedy is made explicit by the narrator. Mrs. Tulliver pleads with Mr. Wakem not to bid for the mill, an option that has hitherto not entered his head. George Eliot exhibits a gloomy view of human nature, though she insists that Mr. Wakem is not excessively evil, merely not one to pass up an opportunity for petty revenge: "Wakem was not without this parenthetic vindictiveness towards the uncomplimentary miller, and now Mrs. Tulliver had put the notion into his head it presented itself to him as a pleasure to do the very thing that would cause Mr. Tulliver the most deadly mortification, and a pleasure of a complex kind, not made up of crude malice but mingling with it the relish of self-approbation. To see an enemy humiliated gives a certain contentment, but this is jejune compared with the highly blent satisfaction of seeing him humiliated by your benevolent action of concession on his behalf" (340).

Wakem buys the mill; Mr. Tulliver is forced to work for him against his will; his miserable anger finally erupts into violence, bringing death to himself and disgrace to his family.

There is a close affinity with Greek tragic irony in the way George Eliot has Mr. Tulliver collapse morally and physically paradoxically just at the moment when his bleak fortunes are turning for the better. Tom comes home one day, not with "his usual saddened evening face" (355), but with "a very pleasant light" in his "blue-grey eyes" (452). He is able to tell his father that he has saved enough for Mr. Tulliver to pay back his creditors. Ominously, the narrator notes, "Tom never lived to taste another moment so delicious as that" (456). For the excitement of the news affects Mr. Tulliver's "active Hotspur temperament" (458) in such a way that, meeting Wakem by chance, he flies into a rage and beats his enemy in a "frenzy of triumphant vengeance" (460).

In Greek drama such events would be "explained" by reference to a man's flawed nature coming into collision with a hard external fate, against which his will is finally powerless. In *The Mill on the Floss* we experience the same complex network of forces, but for fate there now stands a combination of elements, or "composite impulses" (228), these being chance (the meeting with Wakem just at that moment), the behavior of others (notably Mrs. Tulliver), and inevitability according to laws of human nature. That is, Mr. Tulliver's temperament was bound, in certain kinds of circumstances and through agencies partly internal and partly external, to lead him into trouble: "Sad ending to the day that had risen on them all like a beginning of better times! But mingled seed must bear a mingled crop" (462).

This makes it sound as though George Eliot is embracing a determinist view of human nature. And so, up to a point, she is. But determinism implies the absence, or at any rate the uselessness, of moral choice, and George Eliot is very far from taking that view. Human beings do obey involuntarily the laws of their nature, but they may, and should, struggle to get a clear vision of the choices they face. Dorothea in *Middlemarch* achieves this. No character in *The Mill on the Floss* does (though Maggie belatedly sees her error and returns to St. Ogg's, but too late to put it right); the book's tragedies arise out of this fact. Mr. Tulliver's inability to rise above his misfortunes is described in biological terms: "Certain seeds which are required to find a nidus for themselves under unfavourable circumstances have been supplied by nature with an apparatus of hooks, so that they will get a hold on very unreceptive surfaces. The spiritual seed which had been scattered over Mr. Tulliver had apparently been destitute of any corresponding provision, and had slipped off to the winds again from a total absence of hooks" (366).[9]

In mitigation of Mr. Tulliver's wrong choices and, more problematically, of Maggie's, the narrator specifically questions the view that individuals are entirely responsible for their own misfortunes. The following passage has primary reference to Maggie, and its generalized melancholy tone is worth noting:

> But you have known Maggie a long while, and need to be told, not her characteristics, but her history, which is hardly to be predicted

Tragedy

even from the completest knowledge of characteristics. For the tragedy of our lives is not created entirely from within. "Character"—says Novalis in one of his questionable aphorisms—"character is destiny." But not the whole of our destiny. Hamlet, Prince of Denmark, was speculative and irresolute, and we have a great tragedy in consequence. But if his father had lived to a good old age, and his uncle had died an early death, we can conceive Hamlet's having married Ophelia and got through life with a reputation of sanity notwithstanding many soliloquies, and some moody sarcasms towards the fair daughter of Polonius, to say nothing of the frankest incivility to his father-in-law. (514)

Though the narrative voice maintains a bitter humor in relation to the misfortunes of foolish Mr. and Mrs. Tulliver, there is no humor—only unbearable irony—surrounding the effect these misfortunes have on Maggie and Tom. The following paragraph in chapter 1 of Book 3 ("The Downfall") begins with the tragedy of Mr. Tulliver, drawing attention to our duty—here George Eliot's doctrine of realism is invoked—to sympathize with unfortunate millers as much as we would with unfortunate kings and princes. As the paragraph proceeds, the focus shifts to the effect on the younger generation:

And Mr. Tulliver, you perceive, though nothing more than a superior miller and maltster, was as proud and obstinate as if he had been a very lofty personage, in whom such dispositions might be a source of that conspicuous, far-echoing tragedy which sweeps the stage in regal robes, and makes the dullest chronicler sublime. The pride and obstinacy of millers and other insignificant people, whom you pass unnoticingly on the road every day, have their tragedy too, but it is of that unwept, hidden sort, that goes on from generation to generation and leaves no record—such tragedy, perhaps, as lies in the conflicts of young souls, hungry for joy, under a lot made suddenly hard to them, under the dreariness of a home where the morning brings no promise with it, and where the unexpectant discontent of worn and disappointed parents weighs on the children like a damp, thick air in which all the functions of life are depressed; or such tragedy as lies in the slow or sudden death that follows on a bruised passion, though it may be a death that finds only a parish funeral. (275)

Tom's and Maggie's young lives are blighted by the gloom, poverty, disgrace, and death of their father. Tom forgoes all pleasures in order to work off the debt, and he inherits from his father a vicious hatred of Mr. Wakem and everything pertaining to him, including his son Philip, with whom Tom has shared his schooldays at Mr. Stelling's house. Mr. Tulliver's stubbornness has become utter inflexibility in the next generation: Tom is implacable. As for Maggie, she is obliged by her father's failure to leave school and stay at home with her mother. It is the misfortune of a clever girl denied any activity other than domestic. Her only friend is Philip Wakem, the one person with whom intimacy is forbidden by her brother; and her particular form of the Tulliver family obstinacy makes it difficult for her to give Philip up.

Brother and sister are thus doomed, in an agreement between "Greek fate" and modern scientific determinism, to cause one another pain. By skillful plotting and narrative chronology George Eliot sets up a series of clashes between Maggie and Tom. Chapter 1 of Book 5 ("Wheat and Tares") brings Philip and Maggie together as young adults. They talk of books and life, and Maggie feels valued by Philip where she has become irrelevant to Tom. She begins to meet Philip regularly and in secret. The following chapter fills us in on Tom's doings. By hard work and thrift he has managed to save money with the intention of pleasantly surprising the family when he can pay off all the debts. The chapter ends with a significant remark presaging the conflict between Maggie and Tom:

At the time of Maggie's first meeting with Philip, Tom had already nearly a hundred and fifty pounds of his own capital, and while they were walking by the evening light in the Red Deeps, he, by the same evening light, was riding into Laceham, proud of being on his first journey on behalf of Guest and Co., and revolving in his mind all the chances that by the end of another year he should have doubled his gains, lifted off the obloquy of debt from his father's name, and perhaps—for he should be twenty-one—have got a new start for himself, on a higher platform of employment. (423)

Tragedy

When Tom finds out about Maggie's relationship with Philip, he takes it as a deliberate insult to his father's and his own feelings about the Wakems: "While I have been contriving and working that my father may have some peace of mind before he dies—working for the respectability of our family—you have done all you can to destroy both" (446). Maggie gives way for her father's sake, and gives Philip up. But worse is to come. Again George Eliot's timing is precise, bringing painful irony to bear. Tom makes such an impression on his employers by his seriousness and industry that he is finally rewarded by being able to return to live in the family mill. A pattern of exile and return, loss and gain, has been played out: "Between four and five o'clock on the afternoon of the fifth day from that on which Stephen and Maggie had left St. Ogg's, Tom Tulliver was standing on the gravel walk outside the old house at Dorlcote Mill. He was master there now: he had half fulfilled his father's dying wish, and by years of steady self-government and energetic work he had brought himself near to the attainment of more than the old respectability which had been the proud inheritance of the Dodsons and Tullivers" (611).

However, at the same time another, contrary, pattern has been forming. While Tom's fears of Maggie have centered on an expectation that she would renew her hated intimacy with Philip, she has instead been led into another forbidden relationship, with Stephen, bringing disgrace on the family once again. In the paragraph that follows the description of Tom as master of Dorlcote Mill Tom's bitterness is laid bare:

> But Tom's face, as he stood in the hot still sunshine of that summer afternoon, had no gladness, no triumph in it. His mouth wore its bitterest expression, his severe brow its hardest and deepest fold, as he drew down his hat farther over his eyes to shelter them from the sun, and thrusting his hands deep into his pockets, began to walk up and down the gravel. No news of his sister had been heard since Bob Jakin had come back in the steamer from Mudport and put an end to all improbable suppositions of an accident on the water by stating that he had seen her land from a vessel with Mr. Stephen Guest. Would the next news be that she was married—or what? Probably that she was not

married: Tom's mind was set to the expectation of the worst that could happen—not death, but disgrace. (611)

Maggie returns, outwardly the type of the prodigal or the fallen woman, but Tom cannot forgive her. He turns her away from her old home. The tragic drama of mutual thwarting has reached a climax with the rejection of sister by brother. Only the final catastrophe awaits, a death that is also a recognition and a release.

The difficulty of the ending is manifold. In later chapters 1 will discuss the autobiographical impulse to unite brother and sister and the question of whether the catastrophe is adequately prepared for. Here I may note that the deaths of Tom and Maggie are not inevitable in terms of the plot. What is inevitable, and tragic, about their troubled relationship is that Tom should reject Maggie, turning himself into an embittered hermit and her into a wandering exile. This is the logical, if unbearable, outcome of the drama of their mutual incompatibility and the circumstances of their lives. The chapter in which Tom casts his sister out— "You will find no home with me . . . You have been a curse to your best friends . . . I wash my hands of you for ever. You don't belong to me" (612)—makes painful reading (and must have been painful for George Eliot to write).

Inasmuch as the chief tragic theme of the novel has been the clash of natures and circumstances, *this* is the proper tragic ending. The instinct to go beyond this to the *Liebestod* of the flood chapter, while true to the needs of Maggie's nature, is much less convincing with reference to Tom's. The novel has therefore, in a sense, two tragic endings, one psychologically astute (the rejection), the other a product of deep psychological needs on the part of the author (the reconciliation). As Barbara Hardy notes, comparing *The Mill on the Floss* to *David Copperfield* and *Jane Eyre* in this respect, the "solution and conclusions are so visibly needed by the artist, not by the tale."[10] The problem of where to place Stephen in the novel belongs to this larger problem. For Stephen is a catalyst in the primary drama between brother and sister.

Chapter 7

Love and Duty

Stephen Guest, however late he is introduced to the reader and however imperfectly conceived by the author, has an important function. He represents, and argues articulately for, the claims of passion as against those of duty. When George Eliot's Genevan friend D'Albert-Durade undertook the French translation of *The Mill on the Floss,* he suggested entitling it "Amour et Devoir." George Eliot replied robustly:

> As to the title of the Mill, I think your publishers reasonably fear that the enigmatic "Moulin sur la Floss" may be disadvantageous. I have no objection to that title being thrown overboard altogether and the substitution for it of "La Famille Tulliver"—which, by the by, Charlie told me you had decided on when he was with you. I strongly object to "Amour et Devoir," but I have not any repugnance [to] a change for the better. Perhaps it would be well to put "Le Moulin sur la Floss" as the second title—but do what you think best in the matter. Only resist to the death anything of the same [genre as] "Amour et Devoir."[1]

While we may understand her objection to having such a moralistic, schematic title for her natural history-cum-tragedy, there is no doubt that the novel does address the clash of two claims, one of which may be

53

called Love and the other, with qualifications, Duty. The narrative shows clearly (and shockingly to many contemporary critics) how Maggie and Stephen are unable to resist the "Laws of Attraction" operating on them and are "Borne Along by the Tide."[2] They give way to sexual attraction, forgetting the claims of others: Lucy's expectations of marriage to Stephen and Philip's rather more hazy hopes of marriage to Maggie. So described, the issue may seem relatively clearcut. But George Eliot has made it evident that there is no formal engagement between Lucy and Stephen and that even Philip senses that Maggie's statements of warmth toward him are more pitying than passionate, more sisterly than loverlike. (Indeed, Philip is a kind of "enlightened alternative brother," in the words of one modern critic.)[3] That is, there is a duty involved, but it is complicated by being rather vaguely conceived. More important, the passion against which this loving duty is ranged may claim—how modern, this—to be a duty, too, in the sense that it is one's duty to follow an instinct when that instinct is the positive one of love. It seems, then, that the clash may be seen in terms of two partial duties, each related to human affection, that come, unbidden, into collision. Here George Eliot's interest in Sophocles' drama *Antigone* is relevant.

Antigone, daughter of Oedipus and thus a member of the fated house of Atreus, faces a dilemma between two positive duties. George Eliot describes "the turning point of the tragedy" in her short essay "The Antigone and its Moral" (March 1856) as the dramatic collision between "the impulse of sisterly piety which allies itself with reverence for the Gods" and "the duties of citizenship." Both are valid principles, "at war with each." She sketches the plot briefly:

> Etiocles and Polynices, the brothers of Antigone, have slain each other in battle before the gates of Thebes, the one defending his country, the other invading it in conjunction with foreign allies. Hence Creon becomes, by the death of these two sons of Oedipus, the legitimate ruler of Thebes, grants funeral honours to Etiocles, but denies them to Polynices, whose body is cast out to be the prey of beasts and birds, a decree being issued that death will be the penalty of an attempt to bury him. . . . The impulses of affection and religion which urge Antigone to disobey this proclamation are strengthened by the fact that in her

last interview with her brother he had besought her not to leave his corpse unburied. She determines to brave the penalty, buries Polynices, is taken in the act and brought before Creon, to whom she does not attempt to deny that she knew of the proclamation, but declares that she deliberately disobeyed it, and is ready to accept death as its consequence. . . . She is condemned to death. Haemon, the son of Creon, to whom Antigone is betrothed, remonstrates against this judgment in vain. Teiresias also, the blind old soothsayer, alarmed by unfavourable omens, comes to warn Creon against persistence in a course displeasing to the Gods. It is not until he has departed, leaving behind him the denunciation of coming woes, that Creon's confidence begins to falter, and at length, persuaded by the Theban elders, he reverses his decree, and proceeds with his followers to the rocky tomb in which Antigone has been buried alive, that he may deliver her. It is too late. Antigone is already dead; Haemon commits suicide in the madness of despair, and the death of his mother Eurydice on hearing the fatal tidings, completes the ruin of Creon's house.[4]

George Eliot does not draw the usual conclusion, that Creon is a "hypocritical tyrant" and Antigone a "blameless victim." Rather, though our sympathies are chiefly with Antigone, "the exquisite art of Sophocles is shown in the touches by which he makes us feel that Creon, as well as Antigone, is contending for what he believes to be right." There is no solution to the problem; therein lies the tragedy. Is there a solution for Maggie? If not, here is a second sense in which Maggie's story is tragic. Not only is her relationship with Tom so, but her situation with Stephen, which feeds into the antagonism between her and Tom, is also tragic.

How valid in the novel are the claims for love as represented by Stephen? His argument is twofold. First, and this is in accordance with classical tragedy, external event—chance—is partly responsible. George Eliot, playing the part of external fact, has skillfully maneuvered the plot so that Maggie and Stephen, when trying to keep apart because they are aware of the danger of their situation, are unexpectedly brought into the position of going boating together. In one of the many pathetic ironies of the novel, it is kindhearted Lucy who has helped to bring this about, by planning that Maggie and *Philip* should be alone together. George Eliot has Philip's nervous nature so played on by his suspicions of an attraction between Maggie and Stephen that he is too ill to turn up, unwittingly sending Stephen instead, thus completing the fateful arrangement. Stephen argues that "everything has come without our seeking" (590). This negative position is one that Maggie half-refutes: they could have chosen not to go boating, and they can choose now to give each other up.

More difficult for heroine, and novelist, to deny is Stephen's reasoning that the bonds tying them to others have become "unnatural": "We have proved that the feeling which draws us towards each other is too strong to be overcome. That natural law surmounts every other,—we can't help what it clashes with" (601). Here a belief, like George Eliot's, in "undeviating law in the material and moral world"[5] suggests that human beings are bound by their constitutions to obey the laws of instinct. (No wonder Darwin kept mankind and morality out of *The Origin of Species;* how much easier it is to accept that plant and animal species must obey their instincts than that the human species must.) This position is alluded to in the title of the chapter in which Maggie and Stephen first realize their love: "Illustrating the Laws of Attraction." The reference is to the law of elective affinity or chemical attraction, "the tendency which certain elementary substances or their compounds have to unite with other elements and form new compounds" (*Oxford English Dictionary*). So difficult is it for human language to do without the vocabulary of choice that the phenomenon is called "elective" though the two substances hardly make a conscious choice in the matter; Darwin came up against the same problem with his mechanism of "natural selection" in the animal world, and readers were quick to see, and fear, its application to human behavior.

Goethe had boldly entitled his controversial novel, *Die Wahlverwandtschaften* (1809)—known and admired by George Eliot—after this chemical process. It is the story of two couples who are brought into amorous collision. That novel ends unhappily, but the "moral" is left open, for it is not clear whether the tragedy is the result of the indulgence of passion on the part of one attracted couple or of the refusal to submit to it of the other, or indeed of an incalculable combination of both. Goethe was often attacked for the immorality of his novels, but George Eliot, in a strong defense of his *Wilhelm Meister,* argued that his refusal to moralize itself constituted a higher morality:

> Everywhere he brings us into the presence of living, generous humanity—mixed and erring, and self-deluding, but saved from utter corruption by the salt of some noble impulse, some disinterested effort, some beam of good nature, even though grotesque or homely. And his mode of treatment seems to us precisely that which is really moral in its influence. It is without exaggeration; he is in no haste to alarm readers into virtue by melodramatic consequences; he quietly follows the stream of fact and of life; and waits patiently for the moral processes of nature as we all do for her material processes.[6]

George Eliot shares with Goethe an ability to render "mixed and erring, and self-deluding" humanity. Unlike Goethe, she often pleads overtly, through the narrator's voice, for our sympathy with the mistakes and foolishness of her characters; in *The Mill on the Floss* the narrator asks our sympathy for Mr. Tulliver, less often and less convincingly for Tom, and insistently for Maggie. Philip Wakem borrows the authorial wisdom in his letter of forgiveness to Maggie, and his words are strikingly similar to those George Eliot used about Goethe:

> Maggie—I believe in you—I know you never meant to deceive me—I know you tried to keep faith to me, and to all. I believed this before I had any other evidence of it than your own nature. The night after I last parted from you I suffered torments. I had seen what convinced me that you were not free—that there was another whose presence had a power over you which mine never possessed; but through all the suggestions—almost murderous suggestions—of rage and jealousy, my mind made its way to belief in your truthfulness. I was sure that you meant to cleave to me, as you had said; that you had rejected him; that you struggled to renounce him, for Lucy's sake and for mine. But I could see no issue that was not fatal for *you,* and that dread shut out the very thought of resignation. I foresaw that he would not relinquish you, and I believed then, as I believe now, that the strong attraction which drew you together proceeded only from one side of your characters, and belonged to that partial, divided action of our nature which makes half the tragedy of the human lot. (633)

Many situations in George Eliot's novels are susceptible of both a moral and a sympathetic response. For example, in *Middlemarch* we judge Mr. Casaubon wrong in his jealousy and narrow-mindedness, but we pity him because we understand the loneliness and insecurity that underlie his mean behavior. In Maggie's case, all the weight of moral feeling—the narrator's, Philip's, Dr. Kenn's—is thrown into sympathy with Maggie. St. Ogg's "passes judgment," but narrator and readers do not. Of course, Maggie draws back from the brink; she renounces Stephen and becomes a "fallen woman" only in the eyes of society, or "the world's wife" (619). Something curious happens in the novel here. Through the allusion to "elective affinities" together with Stephen's cogent argument and the consistent authorial support for Maggie, we have been brought to the point of condoning their liaison. It is natural; it cannot be helped; it is mutual; to deny it would be wrong; to return to former attachments without love would also be wrong. We are ready to give our assent to the indulgence of their mutual attraction, in spite of our pity for Lucy and Philip. But George Eliot stops Maggie from giving way to the feelings she has been at such pains to show as overpowering. In short, Maggie resists the irresistible. As one contemporary critic noticed, the "picturesque piteousness" of Maggie's situation "somehow confuses one's sense of right and wrong."[7] Sexual morality is shown to be a most difficult question. Goethe, in his novels, wisely refuses to comment. George Eliot does comment, but is finally, it seems, undecided about what Maggie should have done. She declares, trenchantly yet somewhat evasively:

> The great problem of the shifting relation between passion and duty is clear to no man who is capable of apprehending it: the question, whether the moment has come in which a man has fallen below the possibility of a renunciation that will carry any efficacy, and must accept the sway of a passion against which he had struggled as a trespass, is one for which we have no master key that will fit all cases. The casuists have become a by-word of reproach; but their perverted spirit of minute discrimination was the shadow of a truth to which eyes and hearts are too often fatally sealed: the truth, that moral judgments must remain false and hollow, unless they are checked and enlightened

by a perpetual reference to the special circumstances that mark the individual lot. (627–628)

That is to say, George Eliot moralizes about the impossibility of deciding what is moral in certain cases.

John Blackwood read the manuscript in installments sent by the author. When he got to the chapter "Borne Along by the Tide," he wrote to her: "So intensely real is it that I am not sure whether I did not exclaim aloud 'Why the devil is she putting poor Maggie into a position where she would be more than human if she did not come to grief.'"[8] It is an intelligent question, to which we can only guess the answer. We know it was always George Eliot's intention to make Maggie's history tragic; her tragedy must, then, come about through a combination of external circumstances and her own weaknesses—impulsiveness and an unfulfilled longing for affection and admiration. These traits are represented in situation after situation of Maggie's childhood: the need for Tom's love and respect and a fatal tendency to annoy him by forgetting to feed his rabbits, knocking down his house of cards, spilling his wine, boasting of her own quick intelligence. They come into play again in her relationship with Stephen: she is flattered by his attentions. The psychology is astute, and if there is to be tragedy, it must arise from these elements. George Eliot defended herself against Sir Edward Bulwer-Lytton's criticism of Maggie's "whole position towards Stephen":

The other chief point of criticism—Maggie's position towards Stephen—is too vital a part of my whole conception and purpose for me to be converted to the condemnation of it. If I am wrong there—if I did not really know what my heroine would feel and do under the circumstances in which I deliberately placed her, I ought not to have written this book at all, but quite a different book, if any. If the ethics of art do not admit the truthful presentation of a character essentially noble but liable to great error—error that is anguish to its own nobleness—*then*, it seems to me, the ethics of art are too narrow, and must be widened to correspond with a widening psychology.[9]

The difficulty is, as we have noted, that, having committed her tragic mistake, Maggie comes back to St. Ogg's. Her death, a necessary part of the tragic plot, does not follow from her mistake. Moreover, though in the letter quoted above George Eliot speaks unequivocally of Maggie's "great error," our feeling as we read the novel is much less certain about wherein exactly the error lies. I shall return to this point when considering the autobiographical elements of *The Mill on the Floss*.

If Goethe was one novelist whom George Eliot greatly admired, but whose mode of writing about love was different from her own, George Sand, with whom she was frequently compared by contemporary reviewers, was another. Also a woman writing under an assumed male name, also "emancipated" in her relations with men, and also in most of her works a dedicated realist, George Sand wrote several novels giving the woman's point of view in sexual relations. George Eliot read and enthused about these works. Writing to her friend Sara Hennell as early as February 1849, she explained what she owed to Rousseau and George Sand, writers "who have profoundly influenced me" but who "are not in the least oracles to me":

> It is thus with G. Sand. I should never dream of going to her writings as a moral code or text-book. I don't care whether I agree with her about marriage or not—whether I think the design of her plot correct or that she had no precise design at all but began to write as the spirit moved her and trusted to Providence for the catastrophe, which I think the more probable case—it is sufficient for me as a reason for bowing before her in eternal gratitude to that "great power of God" manifested in her—that I cannot read six pages of hers without feeling that it is given to her to delineate human passion and its results—(and I must say in spite of your judgment) some of the moral instincts and their tendencies—with such truthfulness such nicety of discrimination such tragic power and withal such loving gentle humour that one might live a century with nothing but one's own dull faculties and not know so much as those six pages will suggest.[10]

Jacques (1834), of which Elizabeth Barrett, another enthusiast, wrote that the "moral" was "that Love, . . . guilty love, . . . cannot be resisted by the strongest will and most virtuous individuality,"[11] brought praise from George Eliot too. It was "quite preternaturally true" in its depiction of "the psychological anatomy . . . of the early days" of the hero's marriage. *Jacques* was, in George Eliot's view, valuable as "an everyday tragedy."[12] The novel has affinities with both Goethe's *Elective Affinities* and *The Mill on the Floss*. It concerns Jacques, a man of experience, who marries a young girl, Fernande, though he disdains the institution of marriage as an intolerable limitation of freedom. His passion for his young wife and hers for him are frankly and deftly analyzed; so also, as George Eliot noted in her letter to Sara Hennell, are the small mutual misunderstandings and annoyances that sour the marriage. A younger man, Octave, and Jacques's protégée, Sylvia, join the couple, and the chemistry of desire begins to work. Octave, the most thoroughly amoral of the four, feels no guilt at following his instinct to seduce Fernande. All the characters invoke outside forces to explain or excuse their actions—destiny, God, heaven, nature, an "invisible hand"—but Octave puts the doctrine most boldly: "*Qu'est-ce que la vertu dont ils parlent sans cesse? La vraie force est-elle d'étouffer ses passions ou de les satisfaire? Dieu nous les a-t-il données pour les abjurer?*" ("What is the virtue of which they constantly talk? Does true strength consist in smothering one's passions or in satisfying them? Did God give us them in order that we should abjure them?")[13] This is the question put, less violently, by Stephen Guest when he tells Maggie that they have fallen in love despite themselves and have been brought together "without our seeking."

As the story of *Jacques* is told entirely in letters, George Sand is nowhere obliged to vouchsafe her opinion, though the absence of any moral counterargument is striking. Thus George Sand (the "feminine Goethe")[14] seems relatively untroubled by the moral questions raised by sexual passion. Not so George Eliot. She is concerned also to put the case for duty. Maggie replies to Stephen's persuasion about the "natural law" of mutual attraction: "It is not so, Stephen—I'm quite sure that is wrong. I have tried to think it again and again—but I see, if we judged in that way, there would be a warrant for all treachery and cruelty—we should justify breaking the most sacred ties that can ever be formed on earth. If the past is not to bind us, where can duty lie? We should have no law but the inclination of the moment" (601–2).

However, duty, like the passion to which it is here opposed, is a complex idea. It is not a stern, extrinsic law to be obeyed in spite of everything, but is itself bound up with love—love of the past, of roots, of family, of friends. Though the immediate duty of Stephen and Maggie is to Lucy and Philip, the deep love of Maggie for Tom underlies the more recent relationship with Philip. With another twist of tragic irony, George Eliot has Maggie give Stephen up in order to return to being the dutiful sister of Tom, "the natural refuge that had been given her" (612) —though Tom, with his unforgiving and unbelieving nature, is bound to refuse the sacrifice.

The gesture of renunciation may thus seem to be rendered useless, but George Eliot takes a higher view of renunciation than to assess it by its results. Maggie, against the background of a cruel brother and a tongue-wagging St. Ogg's, clings to the feeling that she has, if belatedly and partially, done the right thing. In this she is supported by her spiritual mentor, Dr. Kenn, and by Philip's letter calling her "my loving, large-souled Maggie" (635). The narrator points out that Maggie could have had Stephen "at her feet, offering her a life filled with all luxuries, with daily incense of adoration near and distant, with all possibilities of culture at her command. But there were things in her stronger than vanity— passion, and affection, and long deep memories of early discipline and effort, of early claims on her love and pity" (555).

Duty is thus dictated by love, and renunciation is undertaken through love. At the same time, duty requires real sacrifice. Maggie sacrifices Stephen and her reputation, and gains nothing in return. George Eliot, in one of her clear-sighted essays, had taken the minor novelist Geraldine Jewsbury to task for the "false moral" of her novel *Constance Herbert* (1855), a moral "illustrated in the novel by the story of three ladies, who, after renouncing their lovers, or being renounced by them, have the satisfaction of feeling in the end that these lovers were extremely 'good-for-nothing,' and that they (the ladies) have had an excellent riddance." Here is "neither the true doctrine of renunciation, nor a true representation of the realities of life." It is mere "copy-book morality" in three volumes. For, George Eliot declares, "It is not the fact that what duty calls on us to renounce, will invariably prove 'not worth the keeping'; and if it *were* the fact, renunciation would cease to be moral heroism, and would be simply a calculation of prudence. . . . And it is this very perception that the thing we renounce is precious, is something never to be compensated to us, which constitutes the beauty and heroism of renunciation."[15]

It has seemed to many readers that Stephen has not been shown to be worthy of Maggie's sacrifice, that he never recovers from his introduction in Book 6 as a dandy represented by his "diamond ring, attar of roses, and air of nonchalant leisure" (469). But George Eliot wishes us to believe that after falling in love with Maggie, Stephen becomes aware of a "moral conflict" in himself (469). It is important that we register this, for the essence of Maggie's and Stephen's relationship is that they experience a mutual attraction that takes them both by surprise and that they cannot ignore.

George Eliot proves in *The Mill on the Floss* perhaps more than in any other of her novels that, like George Sand, she can write frankly and perceptively about physical passion. Though it was fashionable from the late nineteenth century until well into this century to think of her as a typical "Victorian," a heavy-handed moralist and prudish preacher in prose, many of her immediate contemporaries were struck, rightly, by her daring and accuracy. The *British Quarterly* reviewer of her early novels noted that from the representation of Hetty Sorrel in *Adam Bede* onwards, there was "a vein of perilous voluptuousness running through her works."[16] Maggie's susceptibility to admiration has been shown many times in the novel—her running away to the gypsies to offer herself as their queen, her teenage identification with the "dark" heroines of Scott's novels—as has her utterly deprived life in this respect. Her "highly strung, hungry nature" is wrought upon by Stephen's attentions, his handsomeness, his fine bass voice. George Eliot deftly demonstrates the psychology of his attraction for Maggie, who has known nothing but rejection or indifference apart from the forbidden (and nonsexual) relationship with Philip. The mutual consciousness of awakening love is described with skill:

If Stephen came in when Lucy was out of the room—if Lucy left them together, they never spoke to each other: Stephen, perhaps, seemed to be examining books or music, and Maggie bent her head assiduously over her work. Each was oppressively conscious of the other's presence, even to the finger-ends. Yet each looked and longed for the same thing to happen the next day. Neither of them had begun to reflect on the matter, or silently to ask, "To what does all this tend?" Maggie only felt that life was revealing something quite new to her, and she was absorbed in the direct, immediate experience, without any energy left for taking account of it, and reasoning about it. Stephen wilfully abstained from self-questioning, and would not admit to himself that he felt an influence which was to have any determining effect on his conduct. (516)

Whether or not George Eliot succeeds in persuading us to take Stephen seriously, she certainly manages to make us feel the romantic thrill for Maggie of the fateful boat journey. Her touch is light but sure:

"Let us go," Stephen murmured, entreatingly, rising, and taking her hand to raise her too. "We shall not be long together."
And they went. Maggie felt that she was being led down the garden among the roses, being helped with firm tender care into the boat, having the cushion and cloak arranged for her feet, and her parasol opened for her (which she had forgotten)—all by this stronger presence that seemed to bear her along without any act of her own will, like the added self which comes with the sudden exalting influence of a strong tonic—and she felt nothing else. Memory was excluded. (588–89)

"And they went." Simple, direct, unmoralizing. Maggie remains passive: "was being led," "being helped," "having the cushion and cloak arranged for her feet." The passive voice, relieving Maggie of agency, extends to the narrator, who reminds us, but gently, of the mistake being committed: "Memory was excluded." The narrator represents the trancelike state of the lovers, or at least of Maggie, by alluding to the regular rhythms of the boat on the water and the harmony of the natural world around. In the following passage "reproach" and "the past and the future" are the only reminders of the moral dubiousness of the occasion.

Otherwise, the scene is given from the point of view of the lovers, who feel as if transported, "enchanted":

> They glided rapidly along, to Stephen's rowing, helped by the backward-flowing tide, past the Tofton trees and houses—on between the silent, sunny fields and pastures which seemed filled with a natural joy that had no reproach for theirs. The breath of the young, unwearied day, the delicious rhythmic dip of the oars, the fragmentary song of a passing bird heard now and then as if it were only the overflowing of brim-full gladness, the sweet solitude of a twofold consciousness that was mingled into one by that grave untiring gaze which need not be averted—what else could there be in their minds for the first hour? Some low, subdued, languid exclamation of love came from Stephen from time to time, as he went on rowing idly, half automatically: otherwise, they spoke no word; for what could words have been, but an inlet to thought? and thought did not belong to that enchanted haze in which they were enveloped—it belonged to the past and the future that lay outside the haze. (589)

Such a passage has a "modern" feel: when put anonymously before students, it is invariably taken to be from a twentieth-century, post-Freudian novel.

There is, then, no solution for Maggie. She makes a mistake that is understandable, given her nature and circumstances. It is not even finally clear what she "could" or "should" have done. We have no "master key" that will fit the case.

Chapter 8

Structure

George Eliot was her own first critic when considering the structure of her novel. She wrote to Blackwood on 3 April 1860 from Rome, where she and Lewes had gone after the last chapter of the manuscript had been sent off: "As for the book, I can see nothing in it just now but the absence of things that might have been there. In fact, the third volume has the material of a novel compressed into it."[1] This was precisely what her critics were to say. Some felt that the last third of the book was an afterthought, but she denied this, explaining how the imbalance had come about: "My love of the childhood scenes made me linger over them; so that I could not develop as fully as I wished the concluding 'Book' in which the tragedy occurs, and which I had looked forward to with much attention and premeditation from the beginning."[2]

A close examination of structural elements in the novel bears out her defense, although there may still be doubts—shared by George Eliot—about her success in unifying the book. The chief problem is, as we have seen, the late, and dubious, introduction of Stephen Guest. Though he is mentioned in passing earlier in the novel, as the expensively educated son of the chief partner of Guest & Co., for whom Mr. Deane works, nothing quite prepares us for his irruption into the foreground in

Book 6. A new tone is adopted by the narrator. After the bitter, pathetic, unfunny irony of Mr. Tulliver's downfall and death and its effect on Maggie and Tom, it is a great shock to turn the page and read the following paragraph:

> The well-furnished drawing-room, with the open grand piano and the pleasant outlook down a sloping garden to a boathouse by the side of the Floss, is Mr. Deane's. The neat little lady in mourning, whose light brown ringlets are falling over the coloured embroidery with which her fingers are busy, is of course Lucy Deane; and the fine young man who is leaning down from his chair to snap the scissors in the extremely abbreviated face of the "King Charles" lying on the young lady's feet, is no other than Mr. Stephen Guest, whose diamond ring, attar of roses, and air of nonchalant leisure at twelve o'clock in the day are the graceful and odoriferous result of the largest oil-mill and the most extensive wharf in St. Ogg's. There is an apparent triviality in the action with the scissors, but your discernment perceives at once that there is a design in it which makes it eminently worthy of a large-headed, long-limbed young man; for you see that Lucy wants the scissors and is compelled, reluctant as she may be, to shake her ringlets back, raise her soft hazel eyes, smile playfully down on the face that is so very nearly on a level with her knee, and holding out her little shell-pink palm, to say,
>   "My scissors, please, if you can renounce the great pleasure of persecuting my poor Minny." (469)

George Eliot clearly feels impelled to move the story on after lingering so long over Tom's and Maggie's childhood. In keeping with the social history that is part of her purpose, she shows how the Deanes have moved up the social scale to join the Guests. But the cynical, playful narrative voice jars rather. Stephen and Lucy are both treated derisively, Lucy being rather too obviously set up as the sweet, insipid little thing against whom Maggie will shine (as Philip says, the dark passionate heroine upstaging the pale fair one). And Stephen is so much the "coxcomb" he is called by one of the young men of St. Ogg's (549) that it is hard for us to accept the narrator's direct plea in chapter 9 of Book 6: "It is clear to you, I hope, that Stephen was not a hypocrite—capable of deliberate doubleness for a selfish end" (552). George Eliot needs our sympathy for Stephen before she sets him adrift on the Floss with Maggie, but because of the compression she has been obliged to impose on the novel at this stage, she has not enough narrative time to win that sympathy. The natural history of a group—a family, the Dodsons and Tullivers, within a social framework, St. Ogg's—which has been so brilliantly narrated in the first five books now takes second place to an inadequately prepared for love drama. (The other love drama, involving Maggie and Tom, does have the continuity and fullness of treatment lacking in the Maggie-Stephen relationship.)

If Stephen is a partial failure in this way, he does have the function of bridging for us the time gap between the action at the end of Book 5 and that at the beginning of Book 6. As a newcomer, he can find out for us what Maggie has been doing in the two years since her father's death. The answer is that Maggie's life had been dull and empty; family finances and her desire to be independent have sent her off to "a dreary situation in a school," as Lucy tells Stephen (472). This is allowable novel plotting. Less acceptable is the emphasis on Stephen's first impression of Maggie, rather too fussily prepared for by a too-cherishing narrator: "'Let me introduce you to my cousin, Miss Tulliver,' said Lucy, turning with wicked enjoyment towards Maggie, who now approached from the farther window. 'This is Mr. Stephen Guest.'" The narrator continues, "For one instant Stephen could not conceal his astonishment at the sight of this tall, dark-eyed nymph with her jet-black coronet of hair, the next, Maggie felt herself, for the first time in her life, receiving the tribute of a very deep blush and a very deep bow from a person towards whom she herself was conscious of timidity" (484). While consonant with the history of Maggie's psychology—her great need for admiration and previous lack of it—this and many more such descriptions of her are slightly embarrassing, reminding us too much of the story of the ugly duckling. George Eliot comes dangerously close to endorsing the grown-up Maggie in the manner of "silly lady novelists" of whom she had made such fun in her essay of 1856. In what she called the *"mind-and-millinery* species" of novel the heroine is a paragon: "Her eyes and her wit are both dazzling; her nose and her morals are alike free from any tendency to irregularity;

she has a superb *contralto* and a superb intellect; she is perfectly well-dressed and perfectly religious; she dances like a sylph and reads the Bible in the original tongues."[3]

Of course, Maggie is by no means so caricaturable as this. Nevertheless, the narrator reminds us often of Maggie's beauty, describing her "dimpled elbow" and "delicate wrist" (561), her responding to Stephen's advances like "a lovely wild animal timid and struggling under caresses" (570); and, more than once, her "bright black coronet" (e.g., 425) and striking eyes—"defying and deprecating, contradicting and clinging, imperious and beseeching" (523). The hair and eyes have been features to which our attention has been drawn during the description of the child Maggie: the waywardness of the hair and its cutting off in a fit of temper being representative of Maggie's impetuousness, and the eyes an outward symbol of Maggie's intelligence, desire for love, and frequent disappointment. The psychological portrait is therefore consistent, but the authorial desire that we love Maggie too insistent.

Given that Maggie is so clearly at the center of the novel's action and emotion, it is perhaps odd that we see her only fitfully. She is prominent at the beginning and end, but frequently absent in the middle. It is Tom's education of which we hear throughout Book 2 ("School-Time") and Tom's introduction to the world of work that occupies much of Book 3 ("The Downfall"). As we shall see, this fact is in itself a comment on the lack of educational and professional opportunities available to girls. Important though that theme is, it entails upon George Eliot a requirement to show Maggie *doing nothing,* which in practice means frequently not showing Maggie at all. It is also the case that for the first two thirds of the novel George Eliot had prominently in her mind the desire to represent imaginatively a whole family's intercourse with the society in which it lives. Mr. Tulliver's interaction with St. Ogg's, the Dodsons as representative of certain features of the town, and Tom's growing up to reach a social position a notch above his parents are all part of the multiple view taken by the social historian of "the general aspect of things at St. Ogg's" (185). Maggie's history is only the most prominent of all the interrelated histories, and it is dealt with, perhaps inevitably, in varying degrees of depth and detail.

After the criticism of the portrayal of Stephen Guest and the intermittent disappearance of Maggie from view, the next most frequent complaint about the structure of *The Mill on the Floss* is that the tragedy—or both tragedies, as we must see the two river episodes, the boating with Stephen and the drowning with Tom—is ill prepared for. This is a criticism that may be at least partially refuted by a close analysis of George Eliot's amazingly tight plotting and her use of devices such as symbolism (water), legend (St. Ogg), and dreams.

So far as plotting is concerned, George Eliot is quite masterly in the way she has Mr. and Mrs. Tulliver act out their tragicomedy and Maggie and Tom their tragedy. She achieves this by means of ironic timing and the clever use of other family strands to complicate matters. For example, Mr. Tulliver's money troubles increase partly as a result of his quarrelsome way with Mrs. Glegg, but are compounded by a mitigating tenderheartedness on his part. Intent on calling in money he has lent to his sister's improvident husband, Mr. Moss, in order to pay back Aunt Glegg, he visits the Mosses. His sister tells him what a good brother he has been to her; this fills him with compunction, the more so as he is rather alarmed at Tom's tendency to be cruel to Maggie. "Poor little wench! She'll have nobody but Tom, belike, when I'm gone" (143). Unable therefore to be hard on his own sister, he changes his mind about calling in the money from Mr. Moss, thus failing to solve his own financial problem. The plotting is skillful here—human kindness mitigates irascibility but helps build up Mr. Tulliver's problems; at the same time a prophetic glance is cast at the future relationship between Tom and Maggie.

Philip Wakem is used several times to push on the ironic, tragic plot. His role in the novel is a puzzling, not to say an embarrassing, one, since George Eliot does not quite exclude a feeling that Maggie "loves" him only in the sense of pitying his deformity, while soaking up his admiration. The narrator hints that Maggie is relieved when Tom ungallantly accuses Philip of taking advantage of Maggie's sympathy "to win what's too good for you—what you'd never get by fair means" (448). There is a suggestion of Philip's unattractiveness to Maggie at the end of what is altogether an awkward chapter describing the confrontation between Tom and Philip in Maggie's presence: "And yet—how was it that she was now and then conscious of a certain dim background of relief in the forced separation from Philip? Surely it was only because the sense of a deliverance from concealment was welcome at any cost?" (451).[4] This hint of honest, if not particularly noble, repugnance on Maggie's part is not further developed.

However, in other ways Philip is important. First, he is a natural foil to Tom during their schooldays at Mr. Stelling's house. Second, George Eliot carefully places his arrival at the school immediately after Mr. Tulliver's decision to go to law against a Mr. Pivart whose irrigation of his land threatens Mr. Tulliver's share of water power, Mr. Pivart's lawyer being the already distrusted Mr. Wakem (Book 2, chapter 2). Thus any relationship between Philip and Maggie is proscribed from the start, given Mr. Tulliver's unreasoning anger and Tom's vengefulness. Further, Philip is Maggie's first admirer; in the absence of proper schooling for Maggie, he is the instrument of her education through his discussion of books with her; it is his argument for life and art that shakes her out of an excessively submissive spirit of renunciation, brought on by solitariness and the reading of Thomas à Kempis. He is the first cause of Maggie's estrangement from Tom, Stephen being the second, and finally, it is his nonappearance that makes way for the fateful boating trip.

The river Floss, the medium on which both crises occur, also contributes to the tight scheme of the novel. It is important *as a river,* since Mr. Tulliver goes to law about its waters and many characters depend upon its traffic for their livelihood: Guest & Co., Mr. Deane, Tom. It is also important symbolically, and it is George Eliot's special skill to embody the symbolic element in the real. For example, Mrs. Tulliver perfectly reasonably and realistically fears that one or other of her headstrong children—probably Maggie—will drown in the Floss or its tributary, the Ripple, on which Dorlcote Mill stands. "She'll tumble in some day" (60), "Goodness heart! she's got drownded" (90), "They're such children for the water, mine are. . . . They'll be brought in dead and drownded some day" (166). This refrain of Mrs. Tulliver's keeps the river as a danger constantly in our minds.

The propensity of the Floss to flood has a real and symbolic function too. The narrator gives the legendary origin of the name St. Ogg's in that chapter in which he surveys the town's verifiable history:

"Ogg the son of Beorl," says my private hagiographer, "was a boatman who gained a scanty living by ferrying passengers across the river Floss. And it came to pass one evening when the winds were high, that there sat moaning by the bank of the river a woman with a child in her arms; and she was clad in rags, and had a worn and withered look. And she craved to be rowed across the river. And the men thereabout questioned her, and said 'Wherefore dost thou desire to cross the river? Tarry till the morning, and take shelter here for the night: so shalt thou be wise, and not foolish.' Still she went on to mourn and crave. But Ogg the son of Beorl came up, and said, 'I will ferry thee across: it is enough that thy heart needs it.' And he ferried her across."

The woman's rags turn into flowing white robes; a halo appears above her head. She blesses Ogg for his pity and kindness, and blesses his boat too.

"And when the floods came, many were saved by reason of that blessing on the boat. But when Ogg the son of Beorl died, behold, in the parting of his soul, the boat loosed itself from its moorings and was floated with the ebbing tide in great swiftness to the ocean and was seen no more. Yet it was witnessed in the floods of after-time, that at the coming on of even, Ogg the son of Beorl was always seen with his boat upon the wide-spreading waters, and the Blessed Virgin sat in the prow shedding a light around as of the moon in its brightness, so that the rowers in the gathering darkness took heart and pulled anew." (182–83)

This account, set in inverted commas and biblical in tone, is entirely mythical, not to be believed, but can be drawn upon symbolically when George Eliot comes to tell of that "flood of after-time" in which the boatman is Maggie, who goes to rescue her brother ("The Final Rescue"), with whom she goes down, to be "seen no more."

Throughout the novel there is intermittent small talk about flooding, real and imagined. Tom and Bob Jakin discuss the "big flood" of which Mr. Tulliver has told his children (103–4). When Mr. Tulliver is faced with having to leave the mill in which he was brought up, he naturally remembers how his father had told him of the "old half-timbered mill that had been there before the last great floods, which damaged it so that his grandfather pulled it down and built the new one" (352). In his misery he is inclined to recall, too, a general superstition passed on by his father: "The old mill 'ud miss me, I think, Luke. There's a story as when the mill changes hands, the river's angry—I've heard my father say it many a time. There's no telling whether there mayn't be summat *in* the story, for this is a puzzling world and Old Harry's got a finger in it—it's been too many for me, I know" (353–54). It is the privilege of the novelist to use such supernatural elements to knit together her plot, while giving them no intellectual credence.

As with superstition, so with dreams. A literary device for conveying translated truths since the Old Testament at least, dream features prominently in *The Mill on the Floss*. Water is again the medium. Philip, after asking his father's permission to woo Maggie, falls into an exhausted waking dream, "in which he fancied Maggie was slipping down a glistening, green, slimy channel of a waterfall, and he was looking on helpless, till he was awakened by what seemed a sudden, awful clash" (544). Maggie and Stephen are often described as semiconscious, dreamerlike in their relationship. Their first encounter without Lucy finds them walking in the garden in a "dim dreamy state" (521). On the day of their elopement Stephen talks "dreamily" (588), they sail in an "enchanted haze" (589), and Maggie is "lulled into acquiescence" (592). She also falls asleep, to dream a guilty, prescient dream, in which in a proto-Freudian way Stephen is displaced by Philip, who is in turn displaced by her deeper childhood love, Tom:

> She was in a boat on the wide water with Stephen, and in the gathering darkness something like a star appeared, that grew and grew till they saw it was the Virgin seated in St. Ogg's boat, and it came nearer and nearer till they saw the Virgin was Lucy and the boatman was Philip— no, not Philip, but her brother, who rowed past without looking at her; and she rose to stretch out her arms and call to him, and their own

boat turned over with the movement and they began to sink, till with one spasm of dread she seemed to awake and find she was a child again in the parlour at evening twilight, and Tom was not really angry. (596)

The river, always the river, is the common factor in the use of symbolism, legend, superstition, and dreams.

Indeed, the novel begins, awkwardly enough though in retrospect one understands the purpose, with a dream. The narrator begins chapter 1 with a description of "the broadening Floss" and its surrounding countryside. A little clumsily, he moves from innocent description to conjuring up "that little girl" (Maggie) standing at the water's edge. Then the picture dissolves, so that the narrator, curiously, seems to offer us something he has "dreamed," something perhaps intermediate between observing (natural history) and making up (fiction): "Ah, my arms are really benumbed. I have been pressing my elbows on the arms of my chair and dreaming that I was standing on the bridge in front of Dorlcote Mill as it looked one February afternoon many years ago. Before I dozed off, I was going to tell you what Mr. and Mrs. Tulliver were talking about as they sat by the bright fire in the left-hand parlour on that very afternoon I have been dreaming of" (55). As Graham Martin points out in an essay on the "unreliable narrator" in *The Mill on the Floss*, this dreamer is wholly different from the worldly-wise, sardonic observer of the Tulliver household in the following chapters.[5]

There is, indeed, a problem with the narrative voice. As we have seen, we are expected to take Stephen Guest seriously although he has been introduced by the narrator with devastating irony. There is also the difficulty, brought home to George Eliot by Blackwood and other contemporary readers, arising from her very success in making us laugh at the Dodson sisters: we neglect to sympathize with them too.[6] As for Tom and the whole question of the narrator's attitude toward his and Maggie's childhood, it must be admitted that the narrator appears to be in two minds.

The melancholy, wise, ironic persona recognizes again and again what an intensely miserable period childhood is to Tom and particularly Maggie *at the time*. Every episode in the early chapters shows

Maggie's high hopes of pleasure being dashed by disagreements with Tom. Most famous is the episode of the jam puffs. Tom cuts the spare one with his pocketknife so that they may share it fairly; the knife "descended on the puff and it was in two, but the result was not satisfactory to Tom"; Maggie, wishing to please him, offers to have the half with less jam; Tom refuses the sacrifice, intent on acting with rectitude. He tells her to close her eyes and choose—"right hand or left?" She chooses luckily. "'You've got it,' said Tom, in a rather bitter tone." Again Maggie offers to have the other. Tom refuses. Maggie eats her half and is pounced on by Tom for not giving him a bite. "'O you greedy thing!' said Tom, when she had swallowed the last morsel. He was conscious of having acted very fairly, and thought she ought to have considered this and made up to him for it" (98–99). All the pleasure of eating jam puffs is spoilt for Maggie by Tom's habit of putting her, and keeping her, despite her strenuous efforts, in the wrong.

Maggie is also excluded by Tom as a punishment for letting his rabbits die. The narrator comments: "These bitter sorrows of childhood!—when sorrow is all new and strange, when hope has not yet got wings to fly beyond the days and weeks, and the space from summer to summer seems measureless" (89). Again and again George Eliot succeeds marvelously in making us feel the bitter disappointments, the intense misery of the child. In a letter of 1844 she had written to Sara Hennell, thinking, no doubt, of her own experience with Isaac: "Childhood is only the beautiful and happy time in contemplation and retrospect—to the child it is full of deep sorrows, the meaning of which is unknown."[7]

Yet the narrator sometimes gives way to the dreamer in this respect. It is odd to have the summing up of the dead rabbits episode as follows: "Life did change for Tom and Maggie; and yet they were not wrong in believing that the thoughts and loves of these first years would always make part of their lives" (94). At the end of Book 2, with Mr. Tulliver ill and in debt, Maggie collects Tom from school and they go home to a morose father and hapless mother. In her eagerness to predict the tragic future for her characters George Eliot seems momentarily to forget that what we have seen of their childish past has been chiefly unhappy (though, of course, rows over hair, pets, fishing, and so on *are* minor compared to disgrace, poverty, and the bitterness of parents). There seems to be no trace of the distancing irony when the narrator says: "They had gone forth together into their new life of sorrow, and they would never more see the sunshine undimmed by remembered cares. They had entered the thorny wilderness, and the golden gates of their childhood had for ever closed behind them" (270).

Perhaps George Eliot is not quite in control of her emotions here, though it is certain that, like Wordsworth in *The Prelude*, she intends to draw a positive lesson about the importance of memories of childhood experience, particularly among natural objects. The narrator ends the chapter on the dead rabbits and fishing expedition with a personal comment redolent of Wordsworth:

> The wood I walk in on this mild May day, with the young yellow-brown foliage of the oaks between me and the blue sky, the white star-flowers and the blue-eyed speedwell and the ground ivy at my feet—what grove of tropic palms, what strange ferns or splendid broad-petalled blossoms, could ever thrill such deep and delicate fibres within me as this home-scene? These familiar flowers, these well-remembered bird-notes, this sky with its fitful brightness, these furrowed and grassy fields, each with a sort of personality given to it by the capricious hedgerows—such things as these are the mother tongue of our imagination, the language that is laden with all the subtle inextricable associations the fleeting hours of our childhood left behind them. Our delight in the sunshine on the deep-bladed grass today, might be no more than the faint perception of wearied souls, if it were not for the sunshine and the grass in the far-off years, which still live in us and transform our perception into love. (94)

Wordsworth, too, draws sustenance from childhood experience, the particular examples of which are usually fearful or guilty (for example, birds' nesting, boat stealing). But Wordsworth is writing an optimistic work, in which both positive and negative elements are seen as working toward the better growth of the poet's mind, "all gratulant if rightly understood."[8] George Eliot's mode is ultimately the tragic one, so that these pieties about childhood affection feed into a melancholy outcome for this particular pair of children. There is, in other words, an unresolved tension between the pastoral, Wordsworthian strain and the tragic in *The Mill on the Floss.* The reason for this ambivalence on the part of the author is most probably to be sought in some facts of George Eliot's life, to which I shall now turn.

Chapter 9

Autobiography

During the writing of *The Mill on the Floss* George Eliot was painfully conscious of difficulties, past and present, in her own life. Though it was important to her intellectually to write—as she had done in several essays of 1855–56—in a Wordsworthian way of the significance of memory and the sanctity of the past, the emotional reality of her life was that she had rejected, and been rejected by, her own past. In the first place, she had lost her faith and become, in Charles Kingsley's disapproving phrase, an "infidel esprit forte,"[1] the translator of Strauss and Feuerbach. This caused a rift with her family and cut her off from her own spiritual inheritance. In a letter of December 1859 to M. D'Albert-Durade she admitted having initially taken up "the attitude of antagonism which belongs to the renunciation of *any* belief." She remembered how angry and unhappy (and guilty?) she had felt when she lodged with D'Albert-Durade in Geneva in 1849, immediately after the death of her father, whom she had nursed and who had previously almost rejected her. Ten years on she could take a larger view of the religion she had lost:

> I think I hardly ever spoke to you of the strong hold Evangelical Christianity had on me from the age of fifteen to two and twenty and of the

abundant intercourse I had had with earnest people of various religious sects. . . . I have no longer any antagonism towards any faith in which human sorrow and human longing for purity have expressed themselves; on the contrary, I have a sympathy with it that predominates over all argumentative tendencies. I have not returned to dogmatic Christianity—to the acceptance of any set of doctrines as a creed, and a superhuman revelation of the Unseen—but I see in it the highest expression of the religious sentiment that has yet found its place in the history of mankind, and I have the profoundest interest in the inward life of sincere Christians in all ages.[2]

This is by way of explaining to D'Albert-Durade how in *Adam Bede* she had been able to represent Dinah's Methodism with tolerant understanding. But the feeling of resentment at her rejection by her father and brother could not be so easily sloughed off. The quarrel with her father had ended, necessarily, with his death. That with her brother remained, becoming total estrangement when she took the second step away from family custom and social convention by her nonlegal union with Lewes. Isaac Evans did not reply personally to her brave letter of 26 May 1857, telling him, nearly three years after the event, of her relationship with Lewes. His solicitor answered for him:

I have had an interview with your Brother in consequence of your letter to him announcing your marriage. He is so much hurt at your not having previously made some communication to him as to your intention and prospects that he cannot make up his mind to write, feeling that he could not do so in a Brotherly Spirit. . . . Permit me to ask when and where you were married and what is the occupation of Mr. Lewes, who I think you refer to in your letter as being actively employed, and where his residence is as you request a remittance to be made to his Bankers in London by the Trustees under your Father's Will.[3]

When George Eliot replied, no doubt confirming Isaac's suspicions of his wayward sister, that the marriage was not legal, no word more was heard from, or on behalf of, Isaac. Under pressure from him her older sister Chrissey and her half sister Fanny also stopped writing to her. As Tom and St. Ogg's in general turn away from Maggie, so Isaac and his family rejected Marian Lewes.

Even the more sophisticated circles of literary London did not show tolerance, and Blackwood, though loyal to her as his best author, was himself dismayed when Lewes revealed to him the secret of "George Eliot's" identity, and became anxious about the likely effect of lifting the veil of anonymity on criticism and sales. Her letters to him after the success of *Adam Bede* and during the writing of *The Mill on the Floss* (January 1859 to March 1860) are full of polite quibbling about how and where to publish the new novel—George Eliot did not want to publish it first in *Blackwood's Magazine*—and whether to lift the pseudonym. She employed a great deal of nervous energy, and Lewes much vigorous activity, in trying to keep the incognito while publicly denying that the wretched Mr. Liggins was George Eliot.[4] Blackwood's insensitivity about the pseudonym, together with his businessman's inclination to offer slightly less than George Eliot and Lewes thought the novel was worth, caused a coolness between them during November and December 1859.[5] But money was not the primary issue. George Eliot's being known to be "Lewes's concubine," the "Strong minded Woman" who had run off with the married man, was.[6]

George Eliot had every reason to be sensitive about her social position, even in radical circles. While Lewes was still invited to dine, his "wife" was often excluded. She wrote bitterly to her Coventry friend Mrs. Bray in 1855: "Light and easily broken ties are what I neither desire theoretically nor could live for practically. Women who are satisfied with such ties do *not* act as I have done—they obtain what they desire and are still invited to dinner."[7] When the Leweses began to entertain regularly at their Regent's Park home in the 1860s, it was mainly men who attended. As the visiting American Charles Eliot Norton observed:

> She is an object of great interest and great curiosity to society here. She is not received in general society, and the women who visit her are either so émancipée as not to mind what the world says about them, or have no social position to maintain. Lewes dines out a good deal, and some of the men with whom he dines go without their wives to his

house on Sundays. No one whom I have heard speak, speaks in other than terms of respect of Mrs. Lewes, but the common feeling is that it will not do for society to condone so flagrant a breach as hers of a convention and a sentiment (to use no stronger terms) on which morality greatly relies for support.[8]

He added, "I suspect society is right in this."

Small wonder, then, that there is a perceptible clash in *The Mill on the Floss* between the narrator's pious remarks about the importance of roots and his execration of the narrow, cruel attitude of St. Ogg's society, including Tom, to Maggie's disappearance and return. As George Eliot knew from experience, society was richly hypocritical, turning a blind eye to the taking of mistresses by married men, so long as a conventional appearance was kept up. St. Ogg's judges Maggie, but its judgment is hypocritical; it is Maggie herself who occupies the moral high ground. There is vehemence in the narrator's tone as he describes how "St. Ogg's Passes Judgment":

It was soon known throughout St. Ogg's that Miss Tulliver was come back: she had not, then, eloped in order to be married to Mr. Stephen Guest—at all events, Mr. Stephen Guest had not married her—which came to the same thing, so far as her culpability was concerned. We judge others according to results; how else?—not knowing the process by which results are arrived at. If Miss Tulliver, after a few months of well-chosen travel, had returned as Mrs. Stephen Guest—with a post-marital *trousseau* and all the advantages possessed even by the most unwelcome wife of an only son, public opinion, which at St. Ogg's, as elsewhere, always knew what to think, would have judged in strict consistency with those results. Public opinion, in these cases, is always of the feminine gender—not the world, but the world's wife: and she would have seen, that two handsome young people—the gentleman of quite the first family in St. Ogg's—having found themselves in a false position, had been led into a course which, to say the least of it, was highly injudicious, and productive of sad pain and disappointment, especially to that sweet young thing, Miss Deane. (619)

Some attempt is made to show tolerance of society's intolerance: "We judge others according to results: how else?" But resentment outweighs reasonableness. The narrator's insight into the St. Ogg's mind shows him that if Maggie and Stephen had married, they would have been forgiven, especially Stephen, for "young men were liable to those sudden infatuated attachments." "But the results, we know, were not of a kind to warrant this extenuation of the past. Maggie had returned without a *trousseau*, without a husband—in that degraded and outcast condition to which error is well known to lead; and the world's wife, with that fine instinct which is given her for the preservation of society, saw at once that Miss Tulliver's conduct had been of the most aggravated kind" (620).

Maggie is blamed by the public mind; Stephen—"a young man of five and twenty is not to be too severely judged" (621)—is comparatively lightly let off. It is the woman, as George Eliot knew, who suffers most at society's hands in such cases. It must have cost her great pain to write in such detail of Maggie's disgrace. Indeed, she told Blackwood from Rome, whither she had escaped after finishing the novel: "I think Rome will at last chase away Maggie and the Mill from my thoughts: I hope it will, for she and her sorrows have clung to me painfully."[9] It is as if George Eliot has been impelled to engineer the plot so that Maggie becomes a social outlaw. Maggie's sorrows and anger are a displacement of George Eliot's own. And Maggie is vindicated—by her own conscience, by the narrator, by Philip, who writes a quite adoring letter to the woman who has dashed his hopes of happiness, and by Maggie's spiritual adviser, Dr. Kenn, who brings her into his house as governess to his children, until wagging tongues make his situation impossible. As many modern critics have observed, George Eliot seems to be determined to punish herself and at the same time to defend her anomalous position vicariously through Maggie. In Barbara Hardy's words, the renunciation of Stephen is a piece of "problem-solving: in it George Eliot transfers the ethical issues involved in her own sexual choice to a different situation which will generalise, justify, and explain."[10]

The whole portrayal of Maggie has come under criticism. Contemporaries noticed the author's "evident yearning over Maggie," and F. R.

Leavis famously accused George Eliot of self-indulgence and self-pity.[11] Maggie has been labeled a neurotic, the evidence being her insecurity, her excessive need to be loved and admired, her childish fantasies of being a gypsy queen and a dark heroine, and her extreme self-denial during her Thomas à Kempis period, alternating with extreme self-indulgence before and after it.[12] The diagnosis is undoubtedly correct, and those critics who, following Leavis, find George Eliot not fully conscious of Maggie's pathology, because it is taken from her own, have a strong case.

As we have seen, the narrator makes little attempt at impartiality in his treatment of Maggie. She is forever being put in the wrong by others, as George Eliot felt she had been, and the narrator is her chief defender. Dr. Kenn, though appearing too late in the novel to have much weight, performs a service for Maggie too: he believes in her. A clergyman whose fellowship is described in Feuerbachian terms as that of "a sort of natural priesthood" (553), he speaks for the author when he tells Maggie after her return: "The persons who are the most incapable of a conscientious struggle such as yours, are precisely those who will be likely to shrink from you on the ground of an unjust judgment" (626).[13] He all but worships Maggie's nobleness of character.

Thus Maggie, though doomed to be misunderstood by most, *is* adored. But not by the one person who matters most to her. From an early age Maggie needs approval from men: her father, Tom, Philip. Apart from the moving moment when Mrs. Tulliver goes with her after Tom turns her away, the mother is irrelevant to Maggie. And Maggie is not shown in any deep relationship with a female friend. Early on, as Maggie is described following Tom around like a faithful dog (to be alternately fondled and kicked like one), we are told of "the need of being loved, the strongest need in poor Maggie's nature" (89). Her father, though far from understanding his clever daughter, "takes her part" in the quarrels with Tom. But from the time of his financial downfall he has no time for her; nor has Tom: "How she wished that [her father] would stroke her head, or give her some sign that he was soothed by the sense that he had a daughter who loved him! But now she got no answer to her little caresses, either from her father or from Tom—the two idols of her life" (371). After Mr. Tulliver's death there is only Tom. Even after the understanding with Philip and the attraction to Stephen, it is Tom, from whom she is temperamentally estranged, whose love she most desires: "To have no cloud between herself and Tom was still a perpetual yearning in her, that had its root deeper than all change" (577). The sentence could have been Marian Evans's description of her feelings toward her brother.

Something happened in March 1859, while she was writing the early chapters of *The Mill on the Floss*, that brought forth her anger with Isaac in a way that must have had a bearing on the complex portrayal of Tom in the novel. Her older sister, Chrissey, died. Until Isaac prevailed upon Chrissey to break off relations with Marian in 1857, the sisters had been good friends, despite Isaac's disapproval of Marian's freethinking. Indeed Isaac, but not Chrissey, had cooled relations with his sister from the time she left Warwickshire for London in 1850. Marian was due to spend the Christmas of 1852 with her sister's family when she heard of the death on 20 December of Chrissey's husband, Edward Clarke, leaving his wife and six children with very little to live on. Marian went at once to help, and clashed with Isaac: "Isaac agreed to let [Chrissey] live rent free in the house at Attleborough, once her own, and tried to be kind to her, 'though not in a very large way.' For Isaac took his position as head of the family very seriously. He always had to have things done in his way, which was obviously the best. After a week Chrissey agreed that Marian could do her no substantial good by staying on at Meriden." This did not please Isaac. As Marian reported to the Brays and Sara Hennell, "Isaac, however, was very indignant to find that I had arranged to leave without consulting him and thereupon flew into a violent passion with me, winding up by saying that he desired I would never 'apply to him for anything whatever'—which, seeing that I have never done so, was almost as superfluous as if I had said that I would never receive a kindness from him."[14]

In February 1859, with *The Mill on the Floss* on her mind, she heard for the first time in two years from Chrissey. She told Mrs. Bray, "I have just had a letter from my Sister—ill in bed—consumptive—regretting that she ever ceased to write to me. It has ploughed up my heart."[15] To Sara Hennell she wrote:

I think her writing was the result of long quiet thought—the slow return of a naturally just and affectionate mind to the position from which it had been thrust by external influence [i.e., Isaac]. She says, "My object in writing to you . . . was to tell you how very sorry I have been that I ceased to write and neglected one who under all circumstances was kind to me and mine. *Pray believe* me when I say it will be the greatest comfort I can possibly receive to know you are *well* and *happy*. Will you write once more etc. etc." I wrote immediately, and I desire to avoid any word of reference to anything with which she associates the idea of alienation. The past is abolished from my mind—I only want her to feel that I love and care for her.

She waited to hear if her sister wanted to see her. On 15 March Chrissey died without a meeting taking place. George Eliot commented to Sara Hennell, "Chrissey's death has taken from the possibility of many things towards which I looked with some hope and yearning in the future."[16] Among the "many things" may have been the long-wished-for reconciliation with Isaac.

Though much of her bitterness and sadness about family matters finds expression in the depiction of the unhappy family in *The Mill on the Floss*, George Eliot gave vent to her most negative feelings in a curious short story written, it seems, immediately after her sister's death. On 31 March she wrote to Blackwood that, while *The Mill on the Floss* would "require time and labour," she had "a slight story of an outré kind—not a *jeu d'esprit*, but a *jeu de melancholie* [sic]." This was "The Lifted Veil," which Blackwood agreed to publish in the July number of *Blackwood's Magazine*, though he obviously disliked it: "I inclose [sic] proof of the Lifted Veil. It is a very striking story, full of thought and most beautifully written. I wish the theme had been a happier one, and I think you must have been worrying and disturbing yourself about something when you wrote."[17]

It is an unpleasant tale, told in the first person by a man who has the gift, or rather curse, of prevision. He foresees only unhappy events, including his marriage to a wicked woman and his own death. He is an unfavored second son, antagonistic toward his older brother. Family relations are destructive, and the marriage tie one of tyranny. The story, unleavened by humor, not dignified by tragedy, is a completely negative piece. Of the relationship between his powerful wife and himself the narrator writes: "There is no tyranny more complete than that which a self-centred negative nature exercises over a morbidly sensitive nature perpetually craving sympathy and support."[18] The remark applies equally to Isaac and Marian, and to Tom and Maggie.

Our knowledge of George Eliot's family preoccupations in 1859 helps to explain the contradictory feelings raised in us by her representation of Tom. The paragraph in which he is introduced begins with the narrator seeing from Tom's point of view, moves into a general observation about boyhood, and ends—though still ostensibly objectively— with critical irony at Tom's expense:

> he submitted to be kissed willingly enough, though Maggie hung on his neck in rather a strangling fashion, while his blue-grey eyes wandered towards the croft and the lambs and the river where he promised himself that he would begin to fish the first thing to-morrow morning. He was one of those lads that grow everywhere in England, and, at twelve or thirteen years of age, look as much alike as goslings:—a lad with light brown hair, cheeks of cream and roses, full lips, indeterminate nose and eyebrows—a physiognomy in which it seems impossible to discern anything but the generic character of boyhood; as different as possible from poor Maggie's phiz, which Nature seemed to have moulded and coloured with the most decided intention. But that same Nature has the deep cunning which hides itself under the appearance of openness, so that simple people think they can see through her quite well, and all the while she is secretly preparing a refutation of their confident prophecies. Under these average boyish physiognomies that she [Nature] seems to turn off by the gross, she conceals some of her most rigid inflexible purposes, some of her most unmodifiable characters; and the dark-eyed, demonstrative, rebellious girl may after all turn out to be a passive being compared with this pink and white bit of masculinity with the indeterminate features. (84–85)

The narrator here ensures our sympathy for Maggie—"poor Maggie"—in the coming scenes in which they will quarrel and Maggie will be blamed. Not that George Eliot neglects to penetrate Tom's psychology as she does Maggie's; on the contrary, there is something brilliantly obsessive about the frequency with which she lays bare the harshness of his nature. Though there is some cuddling and kissing between brother and sister, it is usually at best part of making up after a quarrel. The narrator concedes, "there were tender fibres in the lad" (91), as he describes the reconciliation after Tom's anger at Maggie's neglect of his rabbits. But Tom's negative decisiveness is commented on again and again, sometimes by the narrative voice, often by Tom's own thought processes: "Tom, indeed, was of opinion that Maggie was a silly little thing: all girls were silly—they couldn't throw a stone so as to hit anything, couldn't do anything with a pocket-knife, and were frightened at frogs. Still, he was very fond of his sister, and meant always to take care of her, make her his housekeeper, and punish her when she did wrong" (92). The narrator, in other words, appropriates Tom's thoughts and comments on them in one process. Frequently we are left with a bitterness in our attitude to Tom. Paragraphs in which we see brother and sister at odds with each other end with Maggie exonerated and Tom judged. For example, when Maggie knocks over his house of cards we are told: "She really did not mean it, but the circumstantial evidence was against her, and Tom turned white with anger, but said nothing: he would have struck her, only he knew it was cowardly to strike a girl, and Tom Tulliver was quite determined he would never do anything cowardly" (147).

The narrative of Book 1 follows a pattern in which Maggie's expectation of pleasure dissolves into a fear of punishment and ends in a denial of true pleasure. The fishing trip with Tom constitutes, says the narrator, sombrely enough, "one of their happy mornings." But the threat of Tom's displeasure overshadows even this day:

> They were on their way to the Round Pool—that wonderful pool, which the floods had made a long while ago: no one knew how deep it was; and it was mysterious too that it should be almost a perfect round, framed in with willows and tall reeds, so that the water was only to be seen when you got close to the brink. The sight of the old favourite spot always heightened Tom's good-humour, and he spoke to Maggie in the most amicable whispers, as he opened the precious basket and prepared their tackle. He threw her line for her, and put the rod into

her hand. Maggie thought it probable that the small fish would come to her hook, and the large ones to Tom's. But she had forgotten all about the fish and was looking dreamily at the glassy water, when Tom said, in a loud whisper, "Look, look, Maggie!" and came running to prevent her from snatching her line away.

Maggie was frightened lest she had been doing something wrong, as usual, but presently Tom drew out her line and brought a large tench bouncing on the grass.

Tom was excited.

"O Magsie! you little duck! Empty the basket."

Maggie was not conscious of unusual merit, but it was enough that Tom called her Magsie, and was pleased with her. (92–93)

This is the least miserable childhood experience related in the novel. It leads, rather incongruously, to the Wordsworthian reflection, already quoted, about "familiar flowers" and "well-remembered bird-notes" being the "mother tongue of our imagination." Even this experience, however, is touched with fear and guilt for Maggie.

A similar scene occurs in the sonnet sequence "Brother and Sister," which George Eliot wrote in 1869 and which was published with *The Legend of Jubal* in 1874. There is every reason to think that the events narrated in the poems were taken directly from her memory of childhood outings with Isaac. As Henry James noted in his review of the poems, "Brother and Sister" throws "a grateful light on some of the best pages the author has written,—in which she describes her heroine's childish years in *The Mill on the Floss*. The finest thing in that admirable novel has always been, to our taste, not its portrayal of the young girl's love-struggles as regards her lover, but those as regards her brother."[19] Like Maggie, the speaker of the poem is adoring:

> He was the elder and a little man
> Of forty inches, bound to show no dread,
> And I the girl that puppy-like now ran,
> Now lagged behind my brother's larger tread.

Like Maggie, she is forgetful, and given to self-aggrandizing fantasies:

Autobiography

One day my brother left me in high charge,
To mind the rod, while he went seeking bait,
And bade me, when I saw a nearing barge,
Snatch out the line, lest he should come too late.

Proud of the task, I watched with all my might
For one whole minute, till my eyes grew wide,
Till earth and sky took on a strange new light
And seemed a dream-world floating on some tide—

A fair pavilioned boat for me alone
Bearing me onward through the vast unknown.

As in the episode in the novel, fear of punishment is miraculously changed into (guilty) pleasure at praise:

But sudden came the barge's pitch-black prow,
Nearer and angrier came my brother's cry,
And all my soul was quivering fear, when lo!
Upon the imperilled line, suspended high,

A silver perch! My guilt that won the prey,
Now turned to merit, had a guerdon rich
Of songs and praises, and made merry play,
Until my triumph reached its highest pitch

When all at home were told the wondrous feat,
And how the little sister had fished well.
In secret, though my fortune tasted sweet,
I wondered why this happiness befell.

The poem expresses the Wordsworthian belief in the "primal passionate store, / Whose shaping impulses make manhood whole." In spite of the brother's propensity to anger, "those hours were seed to all my after good." But the idyll—more truly rendered "golden" than the corresponding scenes in the novel—comes to an end: "School parted us; we never found again / That childish world." The ending is obscurely expressed:

> Till the dire years whose awful name is Change
> Had grasped our souls still yearning in divorce,
> And pitiless shaped them in two forms that range
> Two elements which sever their life's course.[20]

The "yearning in divorce" applies to George Eliot and to Maggie, and, though probably only wish-fulfillingly, to Isaac and Tom. The final two lines, however, affirm: "But were another childhood world my share, / I would be born a little sister there." The equivalent affirmation in *The Mill on the Floss* is the cathartic death of Maggie in Tom's arms.

Readers, though unaware of George Eliot's relationship with her brother, felt her bitterness about Tom—one contemporary reviewer sensed the author's "disdain" for him[21]—more than she thought she felt it herself. "Tom is painted with as much love and pity as Maggie," she protested against the *Times* reviewer's comments on the negative portrait of Tom.[22] That he was painted with love we can accept, but pity for Tom is in short supply from the narrator, at least early on. When the pair are young adults, Tom's point of view is given more weight. After discovering that Maggie has been seeing Philip, he is excessively vindictive, dramatically requiring her to choose between Philip and family loyalty, but he is nevertheless shown to have a point when he declares how perverse her affection for Philip is and how dangerous for her father's mental health: "'While I have been contriving and working that my father may have some peace of mind before he dies . . . you have done all you can to destroy [it].' Maggie felt a deep movement of compunction: for the moment, her mind ceased to contend against what she felt to be cruel and unreasonable, and in her self-blame she justified her brother" (445–46). Even here, though, George Eliot does not quite cease to put Tom in the wrong—"what she felt to be cruel and unreasonable"; Maggie "justified her brother," but only temporarily.

Only once more before the crisis do brother and sister confront each other, unable as ever to see eye to eye, and George Eliot again gives

Tom some right in the matter. Maggie asks to be allowed to see Philip at Lucy's house. Tom lectures her, "in the tone of a kind pedagogue":

> "Now listen to me, Maggie: I'll tell you what I mean. You're always in extremes—you have no judgment and self-command; and yet you think you know best, and will not submit to be guided. You know I didn't wish you to take a situation. My aunt Pullet was willing to give you a good home, and you might have lived respectably amongst your relations until I could have provided a home for you with my mother. And that is what I should like to do. I wished my sister to be a lady, and I would always have taken care of you as my father desired, until you were well married. But your ideas and mine never accord, and you will not give way. . . . At one time you take pleasure in a sort of perverse self-denial, and at another, you have not resolution to resist a thing that you know to be wrong."
>
> There was a terrible cutting truth in Tom's words—that hard rind of truth which is discerned by unimaginative, unsympathetic minds. Maggie always writhed under this judgment of Tom's: she rebelled and was humiliated in the same moment: it seemed as if he held a glass before her to show her her own folly and weakness—as if he were a prophetic voice predicting her future fallings—and yet, all the while, she judged him in return: she said inwardly, that he was narrow and unjust, that he was below feeling those mental needs which were often the source of the wrong-doing or absurdity that made her life a planless riddle to him. (503–5)

Though our feelings are, as ever, with Maggie, we understand Tom too, and are told that, unusually, Tom smiled: "his smiles were very pleasant to see when they did come, for the grey eyes could be tender underneath the frown" (506). Overly self-righteous as he is, he has given up any thoughts of his own happiness in order to work for the family name; Mr. Deane hears him say, "I want to have plenty of work. There's nothing else I care about much." The narrator comments, "There was something rather sad in that speech from a young man of three and twenty, even in uncle Deane's business-loving ears" (511).

So there is some muted sympathy for Tom, though always undermined by criticism. Tom is constantly in the narrator's mind. Even in the many passages in the novel in which he and Maggie are apart, his name occurs as a kind of standard for Maggie's feelings, positive and negative. Philip is from their schooldays a brotherly figure for Maggie, a loving substitute for the supercilious Tom. We should know that Maggie's feelings for him will fall short of passion; though he is a more satisfactory brother figure, since he understands and agrees with her, it is Tom to whom she is, unalterably, attached. As Philip says, "you would never love me as well as you love your brother." Maggie agrees: "But then, you know, the first thing I ever remember in my life is standing by the side of the Floss while he held my hand" (402). They return to the topic of brother and sister in almost every conversation. When Maggie argues with Stephen about the prior claims of duties to the past, she is ostensibly referring to her relationship with Philip, but it is the one with Tom that underlies and precedes it. Hence her "perpetual yearning" to be at one with him. Hence the guilty dream in which the boatman is "Philip—no, not Philip, but her brother." Tom displaces the other men with whom she has relations, and her dream ends happily, with her finding (against probability) that "Tom was not really angry" (596).

The scene is set, then, for the cathartic finale. The episode with Stephen is tragic in its consequences for Maggie's reputation and for her self-esteem. It also involves making others unhappy. But the finale, the tragedy which is at the same time glorious, is reserved for the deepest relationship. Tom and Maggie must be reconciled in death, where they could not be in life. Others are excluded from this "Liebestod." Mrs. Tulliver is removed from the scene. "Where is mother?" asks Maggie, to which Tom replies, "She is not here." Then, loverlike, he asks, "Alone, Maggie?" and they enact a scene of mutual recognition:

> It was not till Tom had pushed off and they were on the wide water—he face to face with Maggie—that the full meaning of what had happened rushed upon his mind. It came with so overpowering a force—such an entirely new revelation to his spirit, of the depths in life, that had lain beyond his vision which he had fancied so keen and clear, that he was unable to ask a question. They sat mutely gazing at each other: Maggie with eyes of intense life looking out from a weary, beaten face—Tom pale with a certain awe and humiliation. Thought was busy though the lips were silent: and though he could ask no ques-

tion, he guessed a story of almost miraculous divinely-protected effort. But at last a mist gathered over the blue-grey eyes, and the lips found a word they could utter: the old childish—"Magsie!"

Maggie could make no answer but a long deep sob of that mysterious wondrous happiness that is one with pain. (654–55)

The end comes, and the writing swells to a romantic close: "'It is coming, Maggie!' Tom said, in a deep hoarse voice, loosing the oars, and clasping her. The next instant the boat was no longer seen upon the water—and the huge mass was hurrying on in hideous triumph. But soon the keel of the boat reappeared, a black speck on the golden water. The boat reappeared—but brother and sister had gone down in an embrace never to be parted—living through again in one supreme moment, the days when they had clasped their little hands in love, and roamed the daisied fields together" (655).[23]

No wonder George Eliot wept over the writing of this. The conclusion sees the pair buried together, with the inscription "In their death they were not divided." The Wordsworthian piety about roots has been borne out, but tragically, not positively. George Eliot's own experience did not justify a happy ending; tragic glory is the imaginative mode into which she cast her unhappy alienation from Isaac Evans.

Chapter 10

Education

An important theme, addressed in *The Mill on the Floss* as part of the dynamics of the relationship between Tom and Maggie, is education. In 1859, when the novel was written, as in the 1820s, when it is set, British education still left a lot to be desired. There was little higher education for women until the founding of Girton College, Cambridge, in 1869, though Bedford College in London offered some classes from the early 1850s. It was to be many years later before women could complete their studies by taking university degrees.

George Eliot, who supported her friend Emily Davies in her efforts leading to the founding of Girton, was indignant about the lack of educational opportunities for girls. In an essay of 1855 discussing the work of two extraordinary women, Mary Wollstonecraft and Margaret Fuller, she made a reasoned case for educating women, one which she was also to make in her novels, particularly with reference to Maggie in *The Mill on the Floss* and Dorothea in *Middlemarch*. Her point is subtle: the proper education of women would benefit men (who fear it) as well as women, since it would make women fitter companions for men:

Education

There is a notion commonly entertained among men that an instructed woman, capable of having opinions, is likely to prove an impracticable yoke-fellow, always pulling one way when her husband wants to go the other, oracular in tone, and prone to give curtain lectures on metaphysics. But surely, so far as obstinacy is concerned, your unreasoning animal is the most unmanageable of creatures, where you are not allowed to settle the question by a cudgel, a whip and bridle, or even a string to the leg. For our own part, we see no consistent or commodious medium between the old plan of corporal discipline and that thorough education of women which will make them rational beings in the highest sense of the word.[1]

Again:

Men pay a heavy price for their reluctance to encourage self-help and independent resources in women. The precious meridian years of many a man of genius have to be spent in the toil of routine, that an "establishment" may be kept up for a woman who can understand none of his secret yearnings, who is fit for nothing but to sit in her drawingroom like a doll-Madonna in her shrine. No matter. Anything is more endurable than to change our established formulae about women, or to run the risk of looking up to our wives instead of looking down on them.[2]

Here George Eliot writes from the point of view of men, showing no desire to shriek about women's rights, but subtly seeking to persuade men of the general desirability of introducing those rights. This was always to be her public attitude, particularly after it became widely known that she was living with Lewes. When asked to champion the cause, led by John Stuart Mill, of women's political emancipation, she shied away from speaking out too boldly, largely because of her already difficult social position—"the peculiarities of my own lot," as she described it in a letter of 1867 to John Morley on the issue of votes for women. But in general she was in favor—how could she not be?—of establishing "as far as possible an equivalence of advantages for the two sexes, as to education and the possibilities of free development."[3] In her novels, where she can *show* the sufferings of women as a result of their lack of opportunities rather than theorize about them, the message is correspondingly more vividly conveyed. In *The Mill on the Floss* she makes clear her agreement with Margaret Fuller's remarks about the thwarting of "the desires of little girls" and the "*ennui* that haunts grown women with nothing to do."[4]

In St. Ogg's, then, it is generally known that boys must be educated because they will need to make a living, while girls are merely to be prepared for marriage and submission. Partly because of this belief, boys are indulged where girls are not. Thus Mrs. Tulliver, herself a victim of noneducation, excuses in Tom faults that she criticizes in Maggie: "'My children are so awk'ard wi' their aunts and uncles. Maggie's ten times naughtier when they come than she is other days, and *Tom* doesn't like 'em, bless him—though it's more nat'ral in a boy than a gell'" (96). Small wonder that Tom's frequent taunt is that Maggie is "only a girl." The attitude cuts across age and class barriers. Mr. Tulliver, as we have seen, while delighting in Maggie's cleverness, nevertheless regrets it: "She's twice as 'cute as Tom. Too 'cute for a woman, I'm afraid." Her cleverness will be no advantage, rather the opposite, when it comes to finding a husband for her, or, as he puts it in market terms, "fetching a price for her" (60). Equally brutally, if less colorfully, Mr. Wakem tells Philip, "We don't ask what a woman does—we ask whom she belongs to" (542–43). And Mr. Stelling supports Tom's thoughtless remark, "Girls can't do Euclid" (220).

Maggie's frustrations at having no outlet for her intelligence are an important reason for George Eliot's warm defense of her behavior as both child and young woman. Her excesses, though not always steadily seen as such by the narrator, are sometimes explained as the fruit of unnaturally repressed intellectual energies. Here George Eliot is rather ahead of her time in acknowledging the pathology of mental imbalance in adolescence. We might compare her portrayal of Maggie's daydreams and veerings of mood with the observations of Henry Maudsley, who included in his *Pathology of Mind* (1879) a discussion of mental disorders in girls at the age of puberty: "The range of activity of women is so limited, and their available paths of work in life so few, compared with those which men have in the present social arrangements, that they have not, like men, vicarious outlets for feeling in a variety of healthy aims and pursuits."⁵

Describing Maggie's first meeting with Philip at Mr. Stelling's school, the narrator gives Philip's impression of Maggie, then moves on to a more direct diagnosis of her psychological makeup: "He thought this sister of Tulliver's seemed a nice little thing, quite unlike her brother: he wished *he* had a little sister. What was it, he wondered, that made Maggie's dark eyes remind him of the stories about princesses being turned into animals? . . . I think it was, that her eyes were full of unsatisfied intelligence and unsatisfied, beseeching affection" (253).

When writing about Maggie's frustrations, George Eliot noticeably varies the narrative tone. There is always sympathy, sometimes indulgence, occasionally objectivity, and on rare occasions even irony at Maggie's expense. After describing one of Tom's and Maggie's arguments and Tom's harshness to Maggie, the narrator observes, first with detachment, then a little irony, and finally with indulgence:

> Their mother came in now, and Maggie rushed away, that her burst of tears, which she felt must come, might not happen till she was safe upstairs. They were very bitter tears: everybody in the world seemed so hard and unkind to Maggie: there was no indulgence, no fondness, such as she imagined when she fashioned the world afresh in her own thoughts. In books there were people who were always agreeable or tender, and delighted to do things that made one happy, and who did not show their kindness by finding fault. The world outside the books was not a happy one, Maggie felt: it seemed to be a world where people behaved the best to those they did not pretend to love and that did not belong to them. And if life had no love in it, what else was there for Maggie? Nothing but poverty and the companionship of her mother's narrow griefs—perhaps of her father's heart-cutting childish dependence. (319–20)

Maggie at thirteen is described in one passage with completely conscious observation:

> To the usual precocity of the girl, she added that early experience of struggle, of conflict between the inward impulse and outward fact

which is the lot of every imaginative and passionate nature; and the years since she hammered the nails into her wooden fetish among the worm-eaten shelves of the attic, had been filled with so eager a life in the triple world of reality, books, and waking dreams, that Maggie was strangely old for her years in everything except in her entire want of that prudence and self-command which were the qualities that made Tom manly in the midst of his intellectual boyishness. (367)

This is by way of preparing us to understand her phase of renunciation, prompted by a chance discovery of Thomas à Kempis at a time when "no dream-world would satisfy her now. She wanted some explanation of this hard, real life" (379).

Though there is some confusion in the narrator's attitude to Maggie, George Eliot does reveal an impressive grasp of the teenage psychology that translates frustration into zealous piety, showing how inevitable this is in a girl, who has not the sense of usefulness that a boy enjoys in similar circumstances. Life is hard for both Tom and Maggie when they have to leave school prematurely and return home to a gloomy, sick, ruined father. But at least Tom has "something to do." As Maggie reminds him in one of their brief, bitter, recriminating exchanges: "You are a man, Tom, and can do something in the world" (450). The narrator comments, with the same sweeping melancholy view that he shows when contemplating the superseding of one generation by another, on Maggie's lot:

Poor child! as she leaned her head against the window-frame with her hands clasped tighter and tighter and her foot beating the ground, she was as lonely in her trouble as if she had been the only girl in the civilised world of that day, who had come out of her school-life with a soul untrained for inevitable struggles—with no other part of her inherited share in the hard-won treasures of thought, which generations of painful toil have laid up for the race of men than shreds and patches of feeble literature and false history—with much futile information about Saxon and other kings of doubtful example, but unhappily quite without that knowledge of the irreversible laws within and without her which, governing the habits, becomes morality, and, developing the feelings of submission and dependence, becomes religion. (381)

Education

The melancholy here relates to a determinism only half-embraced by the narrator (who later denies that character is the whole of destiny), and it is the only extended comment on Maggie's schooling. There is a gap in our knowledge of Maggie's growth into adulthood. She attends boarding school until her father becomes ill, but we do not *see* the inadequacies of her education. This is odd, as Maggie is the central character, and her intelligence is much canvassed, but for reasons perhaps impossible to fathom, George Eliot focuses on Tom's (mis)education, not Maggie's. The theme of female education and its failings is left unfinished. Maggie, we see, is ill-equipped for the life she has to live. But an elision takes place between the first two volumes and the third, when Stephen is introduced. In Volume 3 Maggie appears again in St. Ogg's, on leave from schoolteaching (which we also never see—perhaps George Eliot thought Charlotte Brontë had fully covered that topic in *Jane Eyre* and *Villette*), by which time she is mysteriously well educated in her speech and demeanor. George Eliot seems to have let go of one strand of Maggie's inner history—her intellectual hunger—in order to concentrate on the other—her need for affection.

Instead, there is minute analysis of Tom's education. George Eliot shows herself sympathetic to Tom here, as the victim of the wrong sort of teaching, though there is some bitter satire directed against him too—a kind of deflection to the narrator of Maggie's anger at not enjoying the academic education for which she is intellectually suited, while incurious, unintellectual Tom receives such an education, which is sheer torture to *him*. In terms of the family drama at the heart of the novel Tom's education is yet another example of how unfortunate the relationship between Tom and Maggie is. Each is a victim of social circumstances, parental obtuseness, and personal tendencies. Their "education," like everything else relating to them, is the wrong way round.

George Eliot extracts much ironic humor from the situation of an average boy, not academic but quite competent and confident in practical matters, being crammed by a clergyman whose only theory of education is to do unto others as was done to him, namely, to teach Euclid and the classics in an exceedingly dry manner. Tom looks foolish when he is disadvantaged by his accent and his slowness in understanding Mr.

Stelling's heavy wit. We pity him, but we note that the narrator, in a spirit of fairness, refuses to caricature Mr. Stelling absolutely, though making it clear that he represents an incompetent and unkind form of education:

> Not that Mr. Stelling was a harsh-tempered or unkind man—quite the contrary: he was jocose with Tom at table, and corrected his provincialisms and his deportment in the most playful manner: but poor Tom was only the more cowed and confused by this double novelty, for he had never been used to jokes at all like Mr. Stelling's, and for the first time in his life he had a painful sense that he was all wrong somehow. When Mr. Stelling said, as the roast beef was being uncovered, "Now, Tulliver! which would you rather decline, roast beef or the Latin for it?"—Tom, to whom in his coolest moments a pun would have been a hard nut, was thrown into a state of embarrassed alarm that made everything dim to him except the feeling that he would rather not have anything to do with Latin: of course he answered, "Roast beef," whereupon there followed much laughter and some practical joking with the plates, from which Tom gathered that he had in some mysterious way refused beef, and, in fact, made himself appear "a silly." (204–5)

At issue here are both the method of teaching and what should be taught. If Mr. Stelling had taught mathematics with reference to some of Tom's everyday skills and the classics by means of exciting stories of courage and action, he might have found Tom receptive, for

> Tom could predict with accuracy what number of horses were cantering behind him, he could throw a stone right into the centre of a given ripple, he could guess to a fraction how many lengths of his stick it would take to reach across the playground, and could draw almost perfect squares on his slate without any measurement. But Mr. Stelling took no note of these things: he only observed that Tom's faculties failed him before the abstractions hideously symbolised to him in the pages of the Eton Grammar, and that he was in a state bordering on idiocy with regard to the demonstration that two given triangles must be equal—though he could discern with great promptitude and certainty the fact that they *were* equal. (208)

Instead, Tom "scrambles" through, like "many other British youths" (242), on whom the lessons leave "a deposit of vague, fragmentary ineffectual notions" (264). When this expensive and misguided education comes to an abrupt end with Mr. Tulliver's financial ruin, Tom discovers that having been first found "all wrong" when he went to Mr. Stelling's, he is now thought all wrong again by his self-educated uncles, to whom Euclid and the Eton Grammar mean nothing. Tom knows no bookkeeping, and is lectured by Mr. Deane: "Why, sir, I hadn't more schooling to begin with than a charity boy but I saw pretty soon that I couldn't get on far without mastering accounts, and I learned 'em between working hours, after I'd been unlading" (313).

The melancholy irony that pervades the novel is much in evidence here. Tom is not prepared for life, certainly not for the life he must live, though as Mr. Deane points out, "You've had a sort of learning that's all very well for a young fellow like our Mr. Stephen Guest, who'll have nothing to do but sign cheques all his life, and may as well have taken Latin inside his head as any other sort of stuffing" (314). Because of the need for George Eliot to press on with her particular unhappy plot, the question of what would or could have been a proper education for Tom is left unanswered. Since his father had wanted him to rise a notch socially and be equal to lawyers and businessmen, Mr. Deane's wry comment about Stephen Guest might have applied equally to Tom, if the family's finances had prospered. The fact that they have faltered instead makes Tom's education appear, with hindsight, useless *for him*. But, as we have seen, the narrator makes critical observations about the education he receives that are more general in their purport than specific to a country lad who will eventually work in a provincial trading house. The whole topic of education in the novel is one that is dealt with negatively.

It is possible that George Eliot did not wish to take the subject further because she was undecided as to how much a particular education can do to enhance or retard individual characteristics. Would a certain kind of education have opened Tom's closed mind, and made him more sensitive to the needs of others? Certainly the education he does have does nothing of the sort. Tom as a young man is an older version of Tom as a boy: unimaginative and vindictive. External circumstances exacerbate these traits: his lot is a hard one, and acts on his character in such a way as to make him more, not less, intractable. Though the narrator gives some attention to the external facts of Tom's life, the thrust of his analysis is still—as with the child Tom—to judge Tom's character as if it were unreceptive to any influence. Modified sympathy gives way to severe judging:

> there were certain milestones to be passed and one of the first was the payment of his father's debts. Having made up his mind on that point, he strode along without swerving, contracting some rather saturnine sternness, as a young man is likely to do who has a premature call upon him for self-reliance. Tom felt intensely that common cause with his father which springs from family pride, and was bent on being irreproachable as a son; but his growing experience caused him to pass much silent criticism on the rashness and imprudence of his father's past conduct: their dispositions were not in sympathy, and Tom's face showed little radiance during his few home hours. Maggie had an awe of him, against which she struggled, as something unfair to her consciousness of wider thoughts and deeper motives; but it was of no use to struggle. A character at unity with itself—that performs what it intends, subdues every counteracting impulse and has no visions beyond the distinctly possible, is strong by its very negations. (406–7)

As so often in the passages concerning Tom, Maggie is brought in to judge her brother, and we feel that with Tom, more than with Maggie, character *is* destiny. With Maggie, we are to believe that education could have made a difference, though it is not clear exactly how.

The theme of education, though of major importance in the novel, is circumscribed by difficulties. Ultimately, its function is to be among the many elements that further the plot along its predicted tragic path. Positives do not emerge. Maggie's and Tom's lives are strikingly seen as repetitions of an age-old story that has always been sad, particularly for women:

> While Maggie's life-struggles had lain almost entirely within her own soul, one shadowy army fighting another, and the slain shadows for ever rising again, Tom was engaged in a dustier, noisier warfare, grap-

pling with more substantial obstacles, and gaining more definite conquests. So it has been since the days of Hecuba, and of Hector, Tamer of horses: inside the gates, the women with streaming hair and uplifted hands offering prayers, watching the world's combat from afar, filling their long, empty days with memories and fears: outside, the men in fierce struggle with things divine and human, quenching memory in the stronger light of purpose, losing the sense of dread and even of wounds in the hurrying ardour of action. (405)

Certainly George Eliot is angry about women's lot, including their lack of educational opportunities. As Patricia Beer notes, *The Mill on the Floss* provides "a compendium of the handicaps imposed upon women."[6] But the completion of the tragic plot requires that the emphasis move away in the course of the novel from a strict focus on education, or the lack of it, to the particular moral problem facing Maggie.

Chapter 11

Conclusion

The chief puzzle posed by this exciting novel seems to me to concern the nature of Maggie's "mistake." George Eliot appears to offer two views of it. So adept is she at presenting the psychology of the Maggie-Stephen episode—at least as it relates to Maggie—that she partly suggests a condoning of their action. But to carry through such a view, she would logically have to show Maggie and Stephen consummating their love. This she apparently could not bring herself to do, probably for a combination of reasons. It would shock her middle-class, middle-of-the-road readers; it would draw down on herself charges of authorial immorality such as those endured by Goethe and George Sand; it would, inevitably, lead to reflections on her own relationship with Lewes, now publicly known.

Moreover, even if Maggie and Stephen married, though St. Ogg's might eventually accept the fait accompli, a part of Maggie's own conscience—that concerned about prior duties—would not. In other words, in wishing to show us a noble, heroic Maggie, George Eliot has made it impossible for her to behave in a confused and erring way. Or rather, Maggie *does* behave in such a way, but must repent and make a social sacrifice of herself. It is difficult not to see deep desires of the author herself involved here.

Conclusion

Maggie must suffer both guilt and social ostracism, as George Eliot did. But the guilt, like George Eliot's, must be shown to be groundless. In the author's case, her "marriage" with Lewes was entered upon with a clear conscience: Lewes's marriage was already broken. Yet it is probable that George Eliot felt guilty nevertheless. Hers was a social guilt. She believed the marriage tie to be binding, and would not willingly have chosen to break it. Her behavior after Lewes's death, when she married the much younger John Cross, indicated that she wished very much to belong within the accepted social framework of legal marriage. (Ironically, she succeeded in shocking the world once again. Surely there was something unorthodox in a woman of sixty marrying a man of forty?) This deep need for social approval was not satisfied in George Eliot. Perhaps she was therefore unable to accord that approval to her fictionalized representative, Maggie. She could not grant her heroine the marital status denied to herself.

Again, in Maggie's case as in her own, society must be shown to be cruel and unjust in its imposition of disgrace on the woman who disregards its rules. And yet (here is the problem) Maggie herself half-agrees with society. She blames herself and draws back. She is, and surely George Eliot felt herself to be, both guilty and guiltless. Much as George Eliot, so strongly aware of the need for authors to be morally responsible, would wish to be clear here, she cannot be. This is shown in her oracular but inconclusive remarks about the "shifting" nature of passion and duty, the difficulty of finding a master key to fit all cases (627–28). As David Carroll has noted, George Eliot has an instinct to be the sage, while at the same time distrusting formulae for assessing human actions.[1] When the issues of the novel are so close to the painful difficulties of her own life, these two conflicting urges are correspondingly more difficult to reconcile. In the paragraph that follows the remarks about the difficulty of finding a master key to fit all situations, the narrator speaks out for tolerance and a due awareness of the insoluble nature of some human problems. Despite the call for sympathetic understanding, however, there is an edge of bitterness, of not-quite-suppressed impatience, in the narrator's voice that is significant in relation to George Eliot's own experience in her life with Lewes:

All people of broad, strong sense have an instinctive repugnance to the men of maxims; because such people early discern that the mysterious complexity of our life is not to be embraced by maxims, and that to lace ourselves up in formulas of that sort is to repress all the divine promptings and inspirations that spring from growing insight and sympathy. And the man of maxims is the popular representative of the minds that are guided in their moral judgment solely by general rules, thinking that these will lead them to justice by a ready-made patent method, without the trouble of exerting patience, discrimination, impartiality, without any care to assure themselves whether they have the insight that comes from a hardly-earned estimate of temptation, or from a life vivid and intense enough to have created a wide fellow-feeling with all that is human. (268)

Maggie is thus exonerated but also punished. Tom, too, while lovingly presented in the sense that the narrator lingers over the scenes between Maggie and Tom and sympathizes with Maggie's love for him, is at the same time hated and punished. Their joint death represents a displacement of George Eliot's sisterly feelings of anger and unreturned love. As Gillian Beer points out, Antigone is an important figure for George Eliot, not just because her story illustrates the tragedy ensuing from the clash of two valid claims, but also because her great love is for a brother whom she wishes to honor by giving him burial. In psychoanalytical terms, she might here be seen as freeing herself from him, as might Maggie from Tom and George Eliot from Isaac.[2]

Interestingly, though the action of the novel ends with the reunion-in-death of brother and sister, this is not the very end of the novel. As there had been an Introduction ("Outside Dorlcote Mill"), so there is a brief Conclusion. The tragic action is taken up into the natural history of life at St. Ogg's which had been so prominent in the early books. As before, the tone is ambivalent. There is a general sense of progress, of the "onward tendency" of things: "Nature repairs her ravages—repairs them with her sunshine, and with human labour. The desolation wrought by that flood, had left little visible trace on the face of the earth, five years after. The fifth autumn was rich in golden corn-stacks, rising in thick clusters among the distant hedgerows; the wharves and warehouses on the Floss were busy again, with echoes of eager voices, with hopeful lading and unlading" (656). The narrator even reminds us that "every man and woman mentioned in this history was still living—except those whose end we know." Darwin similarly ends a chapter on "The Struggle for Existence" with general hopefulness in the face of some loss: "All that we can do, is to keep steadily in mind that each organic being is striving to increase at a geometrical ratio; that each at some period of its life, during some season of the year, during each generation or at intervals, has to struggle for life, and to suffer great destruction. When we reflect on this struggle, we may console ourselves with the full belief, that the war of nature is not incessant, that no fear is felt, that death is generally prompt, and that the vigorous, the healthy, and the happy survive and multiply."[3]

But, as both authors show, death and destruction are inevitable for some. The flood has made a difference. George Eliot emphasizes this by the repetition of her opening phrase: "Nature repairs her ravages—but not all. The uptorn trees are not rooted again—the parted hills are left scarred: if there is a new growth, the trees are not the same as the old, and the hills underneath their green vesture bear the marks of the past rending. To the eyes that have dwelt on the past, there is no thorough repair" (656). This expression of measured nostalgia indicates that progress is achieved at a cost. Individual tragedies occur. It is hard to be optimistic about human stories of waste, even if one can accept destruction in the animal world with equanimity. Evolution is, as George Eliot saw, a double-edged doctrine.

Everything about her life conspired to make her ambivalent about progress. Brought up in rural England on traditional values in social, political, and religious matters, she found her intellect rejecting them in favor of religious skepticism, political radicalism, and—undesired, this—social unorthodoxy. She had emerged into a cosmopolitan, urbane, progressive world, but she regretted the corresponding loss of piety and tradition, of "those first affections, / Those shadowy recollections" from her past.[4] Hence her "double view" of the lives of the Dodsons and Tullivers as narrow, prosaic, even sordid, and yet at the same time genuine, honest, and perhaps even enviable in their old-fashioned certainties.

107

And when loss of one's roots entails an enforced cutting-off from a much-loved brother, the story that embodies these elements is bound to be melancholy. The wonder is that George Eliot could be so astonishingly witty and humorous in this book, in which she deposited her deepest regrets. It is a truly wonderful book: comic, tragic, epic in its range. And because it is so much a product of George Eliot's psychological needs as well as of her creative genius, it has a specially powerful effect on its readers. In this it may be compared to Dickens's also flawed but magnificent autobiographical novel, *David Copperfield*. Could George Eliot have had the similarity in mind when she wrote to Blackwood in March 1860, saying she did not mean to send a copy to anyone but Dickens?[5]

Notes and References

1. Historical Context

1. "The Natural History of German Life" (July 1856), in *Essays of George Eliot*, ed. Thomas Pinney (New York: Columbia University Press, 1963), 270, 271.

2. See Ludwig Feuerbach, *The Essence of Christianity*, trans. George Eliot (London: John Chapman, 1854; rpt., New York: Harper & Row, 1957), 271, 140, 82, 270.

3. "The Morality of *Wilhelm Meister*" (July 1855), *Essays*, 146–47.

4. *The Mill on the Floss* (Edinburgh and London: Blackwood, 1860; rpt., Harmondsworth, England: Penguin, 1979), 363; hereafter cited in the text.

2. The Importance of the Work

1. Blackwood to George Eliot, 20 March 1860, *The George Eliot Letters*, 9 vols., ed. Gordon S. Haight (New Haven: Yale University Press, 1954–56, 1978), 3:276.

2. Lewes to Blackwood, 5 March 1860, ibid., 3:269.

3. "The Natural History of German Life," *Essays*, 271.

3. Critical Reception

1. George Eliot on Ruskin's *Modern Painters*, vol. 3, in *Westminster Review* (April 1856), reprinted in *George Eliot: A Writer's Notebook 1854–1879 and Uncollected Writings*, ed. Joseph Wiesenfarth (Charlottesville: University of Virginia Press, 1981), 273.

2. "The Natural History of German Life," *Essays*, 271.

3. "Silly Novels by Lady Novelists" (October 1856), ibid., 318.

4. Dickens to G. H. Lewes, 14 November 1859, and Mrs. Gaskell to George Eliot, 3 June 1859, *George Eliot Letters*, 3:203-4, 74.

5. G. H. Lewes to C. L. Lewes, 17 March 1860, ibid., 275.

6. This was Carlyle's phrase on hearing from Lewes about his relationship with Marian Evans, see Gordon S. Haight, *George Eliot: A Biography* (Oxford: Oxford University Press, 1968), 161.

7. G. H. Lewes to Barbara Bodichon, 6 March 1860, *George Eliot Letters*, 3:270.

8. George Eliot to Blackwood, 31 March 1859, and to D'Albert-Durade, 29 January 1861, ibid., 41, 374.

9. Emily Davies to Jane Crow, 21 August 1869, ibid, 8:465.

10. *Times*, 19 May 1860, and *Spectator*, 7 April 1860, in *George Eliot: The Critical Heritage*, ed. David Carroll (London: Routledge & Kegan Paul, 1971), 136, 109.

11. Henry James, "The Novels of George Eliot," *Atlantic Monthly* (October 1866), reprinted in *George Eliot and Her Readers: A Selection of Contemporary Reviews*, ed. John Holmstrom and Laurence Lerner (New York: Barnes & Noble, 1966), 42.

12. Blackwood to George Eliot, 27 February 1860, *George Eliot Letters*, 3:265.

13. George Eliot to William Blackwood, 27 May 1860, ibid., 299.

14. Algernon Swinburne, *A Note on Charlotte Brontë* (1877), reprinted in *The Critical Heritage*, 163.

15. George Eliot to Blackwood, 9 July 1860, *George Eliot Letters*, 3:317.

16. *National Review* 11 (July 1860):214.

17. Virginia Woolf, essay on George Eliot in *Times Literary Supplement* (November 1919), reprinted in *A Century of George Eliot Criticism*, ed. Gordon S. Haight (Boston: Houghton Mifflin, 1965), 188.

18. Swinburne, *The Critical Heritage*, 164; Leslie Stephen, *George Eliot* (London: Macmillan, 1902), 104; F. R. Leavis, *The Great Tradition: George Eliot, Henry James, and Joseph Conrad* (London: Chatto & Windus, 1948), 40.

19. *The Critical Heritage*, 140.

20. Leavis, *The Great Tradition*, 39-40.

21. Barbara Hardy, "The Mill on the Floss," in *Critical Essays on George Eliot*, ed. Barbara Hardy (London: Routledge & Kegan Paul, 1970), 42-58.

22. *Saturday Review* (14 April 1860), in *The Critical Heritage*, 119.

23. Blackwood to George Eliot, 7 March 1860, *George Eliot Letters*, 3:272.

24. In the words of one Freudian critic, "the reunion with Tom fulfills oral and Oedipal wishes. It is also a complex victory composed of a brief rescue, which proves Maggie's superiority over a rival sibling, followed by destruction

satisfying anal rage," Laura Comer Emery, *George Eliot's Creative Conflict: The Other Side of Silence* (Berkeley: University of California Press, 1976), 9.

25. See, for example, Patricia Beer, *Reader, I Married Him: A Study of the Women Characters of Jane Austen, Charlotte Brontë, Elizabeth Gaskell, and George Eliot* (London: Macmillan, 1974); Patricia M. Spacks, *The Female Imagination: A Literary and Psychological Investigation of Women's Writing* (London: Allen & Unwin, 1976); Elaine Showalter, *A Literature of Their Own: British Women Novelists from Brontë to Lessing* (Princeton: Princeton University Press, 1977); Nina Auerbach, *Woman and the Demon: The Life of a Victorian Myth* (Cambridge, Mass.: Harvard University Press, 1982); Dianne F. Sadoff, *Monsters of Affection: Dickens, Eliot, and Brontë on Fatherhood* (Baltimore: Johns Hopkins University Press, 1982).

4. Realism

1. Wordsworth, "I have at all times endeavoured to look steadily at my subject," Preface to *Lyrical Ballads* (1800), *Poetical Works*, ed. Ernest de Selincourt (London: Oxford University Press, 1965), 736.

2. "Silly Novels by Lady Novelists," *Essays*, 302. George Eliot returned frequently to the term "working-day" in her essays, letters, and novels.

3. Ibid., 304.

4. "*Westward Ho!* and *Constance Herbert*" (July 1855), ibid., 134–35.

5. George Eliot to William Blackwood, 27 May 1860, *George Eliot Letters*, 3:299.

6. Emily Davies to Jane Crow, 21 August 1869, ibid., 8:465.

7. "The Natural History of German Life," *Essays*, 287–88. The phrase "familiar with forgotten years," from Wordsworth's *Excursion*, is one she repeats in *The Mill on the Floss*, 181.

8. George Eliot to D'Albert-Durade, 29 January 1861, *George Eliot Letters*, 3:374.

9. "The Natural History of German Life," *Essays*, 278–79. George Eliot refers in this connection to the litigiousness of several characters in Scott's novels.

10. George Eliot dropped "embryonic" for the published version of the novel. The editor of the Penguin edition restores the manuscript reading.

5. Natural History

1. George Eliot to Charles Bray, 25 November 1859, *George Eliot Letters*, 3:214.

2. George Eliot to Barbara Bodichon, 5 December 1859, ibid., 227.

3. George Eliot's reference is to W. J. Broderip, *Leaves from the Note Book of a Naturalist* (1852).

4. Charles Darwin, *The Origin of Species* (London: John Murray, 1859), ed. with an introduction by J. W. Burrow (Harmondsworth: Penguin, 1986), 170–71.

5. G. H. Lewes, Conclusion to *Sea-Side Studies* (Edinburgh and London: Blackwood, 1858), 397.

6. Blackwood to George Eliot, 3 and 9 February 1860, *George Eliot Letters*, 3:256, 259.

7. The editor of the Penguin edition has restored the original wording.

8. Blackwood to George Eliot, 15 June 1860, *George Eliot Letters*, 3:305.

9. For an interesting discussion of this topic see Gillian Beer, *Darwin's Plots: Evolutionary Narrative in Darwin, George Eliot and Nineteenth-Century Fiction* (London: Routledge & Kegan Paul, 1983).

10. G. H. Lewes, *Sea-Side Studies*, 397.

11. Darwin, *On the Origin of Species*, 459.

12. Ibid., 263.

13. The Penguin edition prints the manuscript version, 320.

6. Tragedy

1. See the letters between George Eliot and Blackwood, 3–6 January 1860, *George Eliot Letters*, 3:240–45.

2. *Guardian* (25 April 1860), in *The Critical Heritage*, 127; Walter Allen, *George Eliot* (New York: Macmillan, 1964), 116.

3. Wiesenfarth, ed., *George Eliot: a Writer's Notebook*, xxiii–xxiv, 36ff.

4. The phrase to describe the long growth and history of the town, "like a millennial tree," has affinities with Darwin's famous likening of natural selection through the ages to the ramifications of "a great tree," *The Origin of Species*, 171–72.

5. George Eliot to Blackwood, 9 July 1860, *George Eliot Letters*, 3:317.

6. See George Eliot to Blackwood, 3 January 1860, ibid., 240.

7. See Emily Davies to Jane Crow, recording a conversation with George Eliot, 21 August 1869, ibid., 8:465–66.

8. *Adam Bede* (Edinburgh and London: Blackwood, 1859; reprint, Harmondsworth: Penguin, 1980), 83–84.

9. Compare G. H. Lewes, *Studies in Animal Life* (London: Smith, Elder, 1862), on the larva of a common gnat, which "leads an active predatory life,

jerking through the water, and fastening to the stems of weed or sides of the jar by means of the tiny hooks at the end of its tail," 52.

10. Hardy, *Critical Essays*, 44.

7. Love and Duty

1. George Eliot to D'Albert-Durade, 28 November 1862, *George Eliot Letters*, 4:68–69.

2. These are the titles of chapters 6 and 13 of Book 6, "The Great Temptation."

3. Ian Adam, "The Ambivalence of *The Mill on the Floss*", in *George Eliot: A Centenary Tribute*, ed. Gordon S. Haight and Rosemary T. VanArsdel (Totowa, N. J.: Barnes & Noble, 1982), 133.

4. "The Antigone and its Moral" (March 1856), *Essays*, 263–64.

5. See George Eliot's article, "The Progress of the Intellect" (January 1851), ibid., 31.

6. "The Morality of *Wilhelm Meister*" (July 1855), ibid., 146–47.

7. Dinah Moluck in *Macmillan's Magazine* (April 1860), in *The Critical Heritage*, 157.

8. Blackwood to George Eliot, 7 March 1860, *George Eliot Letters*, 3:272.

9. George Eliot to Blackwood, 9 July 1860, ibid., 317–18.

10. George Eliot to Sara Hennell, 9 February 1849, ibid., 1:277–78. See Patricia Thomson, *George Sand and the Victorians: Her Influence and Reputation in Nineteenth-Century England* (London: Macmillan, 1977), 152ff., for an account of George Sand's importance for George Eliot.

11. Elizabeth Barrett to Miss Mitford, 1 October 1844, in Betty Miller, *Elizabeth Barrett to Miss Mitford* (London: John Murray, 1954), 227–28.

12. George Eliot to Sara Hennell, 9 February 1849, *George Eliot Letters*, 1:277.

13. George Sand, *Jacques* (1834), in *Oeuvres de George Sand*, Nouvelle Edition revue par l'auteur (Paris: Perrotin, 1844), 274.

14. So described by F. W. H. Myers, "George Sand," *Nineteenth Century* 1 (April 1877):229.

15. "*Westward Ho!* and *Constance Herbert*" (July 1855), *Essays*, 134–35.

16. *British Quarterly Review* (January 1867), quoted in *The Critical Heritage*, 11.

8. Structure

1. George Eliot to Blackwood, 3 April 1860, *George Eliot Letters*, 3:285.

2. George Eliot to D'Albert-Durade, 29 January 1861, ibid., 374.

3. "Silly Novels by Lady Novelists" (October 1856), *Essays*, 302.

4. George Eliot admitted that the chapter was not successful; see her letter to Blackwood, 9 July 1860, *George Eliot Letters*, 3:317.

5. Graham Martin, "*The Mill on the Floss* and The Unreliable Narrator," in *George Eliot: Centenary Essays and an Unpublished Fragment*, ed. Anne Smith (London: Vision Press, 1980), 36ff.

6. See George Eliot to William Blackwood, 27 May 1860, *George Eliot Letters*, 3:299.

7. George Eliot to Sara Hennell, 3 March 1844, ibid., 1:173.

8. Wordsworth, *The Prelude* (1805), Book 13, line 385, in *William Wordsworth: The Prelude 1799, 1805, 1850*, ed. Jonathan Wordsworth, M. H. Abrams, Stephen Gill (New York: W. W. Norton, 1979), 478.

9. Autobiography

1. Charles Kingsley to F. D. Maurice in 1857, R. B. Martin, *The Dust of Combat: A Life of Charles Kingsley* (London: Faber & Faber, 1959), 181.

2. George Eliot to D'Albert-Durade, 6 December 1859, *George Eliot Letters*, 3:230–31.

3. Vincent Holbeche to George Eliot, 9 June 1857, ibid., 2:346.

4. See Haight, *George Eliot: A Biography*, 231ff.

5. For details of the complicated story of Liggins, see *George Eliot Letters*, 3:190–236.

6. Charles Kingsley to F. D. Maurice, R. B. Martin, *The Dust of Combat*, 181; Thomas Carlyle noted at the bottom of an explanatory letter from Lewes that he would not answer on the subject of the "strong minded woman," see Haight, *George Eliot: A Biography*, 161.

7. George Eliot to Mrs. Bray, 4 September 1855, *George Eliot Letters*, 2:214.

8. Haight, *George Eliot: A Biography*, 409.

9. George Eliot to Blackwood, 3 April 1860, *George Eliot Letters*, 3:285.

10. Hardy, *Critical Essays*, 50.

11. Dinah Mulock, *Macmillan's Magazine, The Critical Heritage*, 157; Leavis, *The Great Tradition*, 42.

12. See Bernard J. Paris, *A Psychological Approach to Fiction* (Bloomington: Indiana University Press, 1974). See also Patricia Thomson, *George Sand and the Victorians*, for the persuasive argument that the young Maggie shares her pious phase not only with the young Mary Ann Evans but also with the young George Sand, as described in Sand's autobiography, which George Eliot knew.

13. The words "on the ground of an unjust judgment" appear in the manuscript but not in the published version of the novel. Perhaps George Eliot realized she was exposing too directly her own bitterness in the deleted phrase. The Penguin editor restores it.

14. Haight, *George Eliot: A Biography*, 125; *George Eliot Letters*, 2:75.

15. George Eliot to Mrs. Bray, 24 February 1859, ibid., 3:23.

16. George Eliot to Sara Hennell, 26 February and 21 March 1859, ibid., 26, 28.

17. George Eliot to Blackwood, 31 March 1859, and Blackwood to George Eliot, 18 May 1859, ibid., 41, 67.

18. *The Lifted Veil (Blackwood's Magazine*, July 1859; reprint, London: Virago Press, 1985), 22.

19. Henry James in *North American Review* (October 1874), reprinted in *A Century of George Eliot Criticism*, 89.

20. "Brother and Sister," *The Legend of Jubal and Other Poems* (Edinburgh and London: Blackwood, 1874), 209–19.

21. Dinah Mulock in *Macmillan's Magazine, The Critical Heritage*, 157.

22. George Eliot to William Blackwood, 27 May 1860, *George Eliot Letters*, 3:299.

23. Gillian Beer refers to this scene as "orgasmic," *George Eliot* (Brighton: Harvester Press, 1986), 102.

10. Education

1. "Margaret Fuller and Mary Wollstonecraft" (October 1855), *Essays*, 203.

2. Ibid., 204–5.

3. George Eliot to John Morley, 14 May 1867, *George Eliot Letters*, 8:402.

4. Quoted by George Eliot from Margaret Fuller's *Woman in the Nineteenth Century* (1855), *Essays*, 204.

5. Henry Maudsley, *The Pathology of Mind* (London: Macmillan, 1879), 450. Maudsley goes on to describe the behavior in some extreme cases as "involuntarily wilful" (450–51), which is an apt description of Maggie.

6. Patricia Beer, *Reader, I Married Him*, 189—90.

11. Conclusion

1. David Carroll, "The Sybil of Mercia," *Studies in the Novel* 15 (1983):10ff.

2. Gillian Beer, *George Eliot*, 94–95.

3. Darwin, *The Origin of Species*, 129.
4. Wordsworth, "Immortality Ode," *Poetical Works*, 461.
5. George Eliot to Blackwood, 22 March 1860, *George Eliot Letters*, 3:279.

Selected Bibliography

Primary Works

Adam Bede. Edinburgh and London: Blackwood, 1859; reprinted, Harmondsworth, England: Penguin, 1980.

"Brother and Sister." In *The Legend of Jubal and Other Poems*. Edinburgh and London: Blackwood, 1874.

The Lifted Veil. *Blackwood's Magazine*, July 1859; reprinted, London: Virago Press, 1985.

Middlemarch. Edinburgh and London: Blackwood, 1873; reprinted, Harmondsworth, England: Penguin, 1965.

The Mill on the Floss. Edinburgh and London: Blackwood, 1860; reprinted, Harmondsworth, England: Penguin, 1979.

Scenes of Clerical Life. Edinburgh and London: Blackwood, 1858; reprinted, Harmondsworth, England: Penguin, 1973.

Essays of George Eliot. Edited by Thomas Pinney. New York: Columbia University Press, 1963.

The George Eliot Letters. Edited by Gordon S. Haight. 9 vols. New Haven: Yale University Press, 1954–56, 1978.

George Eliot: A Writer's Notebook 1854–1879 and Uncollected Writings. Edited by Joseph Wiesenfarth. Charlottesville: Virginia University Press, 1981.

The Essence of Christianity, by Ludwig Feuerbach. Translated by George Eliot. London: John Chapman, 1854; reprinted, New York: Harper & Row, 1957.

Secondary Works

Books and Parts of Books

Adam, Ian. "The Ambivalence of *The Mill on the Floss*." In *George Eliot: A*

Centenary Tribute, edited by Gordon S. Haight and Rosemary T. VanArsdel. Totowa, N.J.: Barnes & Noble, 1982. A useful essay on the shifting point of view and the Wordsworthian element in *The Mill on the Floss.*

Allen, Walter. *George Eliot.* New York: Macmillan, 1964. A general life and works, now rather out of date.

Auerbach, Nina. *Woman and the Demon: The Life of a Victorian Myth.* Cambridge, Mass.: Harvard University Press, 1982. A general survey on the topic of women in Victorian literature, with passing references to *The Mill on the Floss.* Good illustrations from Victorian paintings and drawings.

Beer, Gillian. *Darwin's Plots: Evolutionary Narrative in Darwin, George Eliot and Nineteenth-Century Fiction.* London: Routledge & Kegan Paul, 1983. An interesting work linking Victorian science and literature, with particular reference to George Eliot (though not *The Mill on the Floss*) and Hardy.

_____. *George Eliot.* Brighton: Harvester Press, 1986. A feminist study of George Eliot's novels in the Key Women Writers series.

Beer, Patricia. *Reader, I Married Him: A Study of the Women Characters of Jane Austen, Charlotte Brontë, Elizabeth Gaskell, and George Eliot.* London: Macmillan, 1974. An influential feminist study of Victorian women writers.

Bonaparte, Felicia. *Will and Destiny: Morality and Tragedy in George Eliot's Novels.* New York: New York University Press, 1975. As its title suggests, a study of George Eliot's use of themes and categories familiar in classical tragedy and transformed according to her intellectual and moral concerns.

Carroll, David, ed. *George Eliot: The Critical Heritage.* London: Routledge & Kegan Paul, 1971. Compendium of articles on George Eliot's novels, from contemporary critics to the twentieth century. Excellent introduction by David Carroll.

Darwin, Charles. *The Origin of Species by Means of Natural Selection, or The Preservation of Favoured Races in the Struggle for Life.* London: John Murray, 1859; reprinted, Harmondsworth, England: Penguin, 1986.

Emery, Laura Comer. *George Eliot's Creative Conflict: The Other Side of Silence.* Berkeley: University of California Press, 1976. A Freudian analysis of George Eliot's novels, seeing *The Mill on the Floss* in terms of "inadequately controlled fantasy" necessary to George Eliot's development toward mature control of fantasy in *Middlemarch.* Interesting, if schematic.

Haight, Gordon S. *George Eliot: A Biography.* Oxford: Oxford University Press, 1968, reprinted 1969. The standard scholarly biography of George Eliot.

_____, ed. *A Century of George Eliot Criticism.* Boston: Houghton Mifflin, 1965. Useful selection of criticism on George Eliot, 1858–1962.

Hardy, Barbara. "The Mill on the Floss." In *Critical Essays on George Eliot,* edited by Barbara Hardy. London: Routledge & Kegan Paul, 1970. Good close critical reading of the novel, relating its problems to the facts of George Eliot's life.

Holmstrom, John, and Laurence Lerner, eds. *George Eliot and Her Readers: A Selection of Contemporary Reviews.* New York: Barnes & Noble, 1966. A helpful selection of the best Victorian criticism of George Eliot.

Leavis, F. R. *The Great Tradition: George Eliot, Henry James, and Joseph Conrad.* London: Chatto & Windus, 1948. Influential in the rehabilitation of George Eliot's reputation generally, this book finds fault with her portrayal of Maggie in *The Mill on the Floss.*

Lewes, G. H. *Sea-side Studies at Ilfracombe, Tenby, the Scilly Isles and Jersey.* Edinburgh and London: Blackwood, 1858.

_____. *Studies in Animal Life.* London: Smith, Elder & Co., 1862.

Martin, Graham. "*The Mill on the Floss* and The Unreliable Narrator." In *George Eliot: Centenary Essays and An Unpublished Fragment*, edited by Anne Smith. London: Vision Press, 1980. Good essay on the narrator's ambivalence.

Martin, Robert Bernard. *The Dust of Combat: A Life of Charles Kingsley.* London: Faber & Faber, 1959.

Maudsley, Henry. *The Pathology of Mind.* London: Macmillan, 1879.

Miller, Betty. *Elizabeth Barrett to Miss Mitford.* London: John Murray, 1954.

Paris, Bernard J. *A Psychological Approach to Fiction.* Bloomington: Indiana University Press, 1974. Includes a chapter on "The Inner Conflicts of Maggie Tulliver," analyzing Maggie's neurotic behavior.

Sadoff, Dianne F. *Monsters of Affection: Dickens, Eliot, and Brontë on Fatherhood.* Baltimore: Johns Hopkins University Press, 1982. Has one chapter on the relations between George Eliot's heroines and their fathers.

Sand, George. *Jacques.* 1834; revised edition, *Oeuvres de George Sand.* Paris: Perrotin, 1844.

Showalter, Elaine. *A Literature of Their Own: British Women Novelists from Brontë to Lessing.* Princeton: Princeton University Press, 1977. Important feminist study, though dealing with George Eliot only intermittently.

Spacks, Patricia M. *The Female Imagination: A Literary and Psychological Investigation of Women's Writing.* London: Allen & Unwin, 1976. Has a few pages on the topic of women in *The Mill on the Floss.*

Stephen, Leslie. *George Eliot.* London: Macmillan, 1902. Good lively criticism in the English Men of Letters series.

Thomson, Patricia. *George Sand and the Victorians: Her Influence and Reputation in Nineteenth-Century England.* London: Macmillan, 1977. An excellent study, making a cogent case for the widespread interest shown by Victorian authors in George Sand's life and works.

Wordsworth, William. *Poetical Works*. Edited by Ernest de Selincourt. London: Oxford University Press, 1965.

————. *The Prelude 1799, 1805, 1850*. Edited by Jonathan Wordsworth, M. H. Abrams, Stephen Gill. New York: W. W. Norton, 1979.

Journal Articles

Carroll, David. "The Sybil of Mercia." *Studies in the Novel* 15 (1983):10–23. An astute study of George Eliot's reputation as a female sage.

Myers, F. W. H. "George Sand." *Nineteenth Century* 1 (April 1877):221–41.

Index

Index

About the Author

Rosemary Ashton was educated at the universities of Aberdeen, Heidelberg, and Cambridge and teaches at University College London, where she is reader in English literature. She is the author of *The German Idea: Four English Writers and the Reception of German Thought 1800–1850* (1980), *George Eliot* (1983), and *Little Germany: Exile and Asylum in Victorian England* (1986). She has also edited and introduced Susan Ferrier's *Marriage* (1986), Mrs. Humphry Ward's *Robert Elsmere* (1987), and J. A. Froude's *The Nemesis of Faith* (1988).

Ashton is at present a British Academy research reader, working on a biography of G. H. Lewes. She is married, with three children, and lives in London.